KENTUCKY
PASSION

KENTUCKY

WILDCAT WISDOM AND INSPIRATION

PASSION

DEL DUDUIT *and* **DR. JOHN HUANG**

RED ⚡ LIGHTNING BOOKS

This book is a publication of

Red Lightning Books
1320 East 10th Street
Bloomington, Indiana 47405 USA

redlightningbooks.com

© 2021 by Del Duduit and John Huang

Manufactured in the United States of America

First printing 2021

ISBN 978-1-68435-165-7 (hdbk.)
ISBN 978-1-68435-166-4 (pbk.)
ISBN 978-1-68435-167-1 (web PDF)

From Del:
I would like to dedicate this book to
my first sports editor, Jim Wharton, who gave me
a shot as a sportswriter. Thank you.

From John:
My love affair with Kentucky Basketball began
long before I enrolled at the university. But it wasn't
until I graduated that I felt fully invested. My eleven years
attending UK would never have been possible without the
love, encouragement, and support of my parents.
Pete and Jane Huang—this one's for you.

CONTENTS

ACKNOWLEDGMENTS

THE FOLLOWING PEOPLE PLAYED A key role in this book.

Thank you to my wife, Angie, for your love and dedication and for taking the time to be the first editor on this project.

Thank you to my agent, Cyle Young, for your guidance and support.

Thank you to Dave Hulsey, Anna Francis, and the entire team at Indiana University Press for your hard work.

Thank you, John Huang, for being a fantastic coauthor and a good friend. Your superior knowledge of and passion for Kentucky Basketball guided and inspired me throughout this project.

Go Cats.

Del

THANKS TO MY AGENT, CYLE YOUNG, for this exciting opportunity. Thanks also to Dave Hulsey, Anna Francis, and all the fine folks at Indiana University Press for this near-spiritual experience.

Thanks to Dr. Michael Huang (https://drmikephotos.smug mug.com/) for allowing us to include his wonderful photos in this book.

Thank you to my coauthor, Del Duduit, for writing this book with me. I appreciate your guidance and expertise. Most importantly, I'm thankful for our friendship.

Go Cats!

John

FOREWORD

Kyle Macy

UNIVERSITY OF KENTUCKY BASKETBALL FANS are PAS-
SIONATE about their team. They absolutely love their Wildcats.
Not once since I first stepped out on the floor of Rupp Arena has
that passion ever waned. Whether Joe B. Hall, Eddie Sutton,
Rick Pitino, Tubby Smith, Billy Gillispie, or John Calipari was
coaching the team, Big Blue Nation always showed up in force
to cheer them on.

Over the years, I've been privileged to meet a lot of Kentucky
fans. I can confirm that their passion runs deep. Wildcat fans
are radically different. They don't just watch their teams play—
they're completely devoted to the players, the program, and the
university itself. UK fans take the history and tradition of the
Big Blue seriously, and they wear it proudly over their hearts 365
days a year, wherever they may be.

As part of UK's 1978 national championship team, I've been
the subject of numerous Kentucky Basketball books. I've writ-
ten a couple of them myself. So I know full well the enthusiasm
that exists within the borders of the commonwealth. Ever since
I wore the uniform, I've been on the lookout for a book that
perfectly captures the passion of the entire program.

John Huang and Del Duduit have done what no one else has yet to accomplish. In *Kentucky Passion*, they've taken some of the most memorable players and iconic moments of Kentucky Basketball and packaged them in a labor of love. Together with John's brother, Michael—a heck of a photographer in his own right—they've produced the quintessential masterpiece of Wildcat Basketball lore. Not only do the carefully crafted pages capture the essence of all these historical on-court moments, but they also leave you with a flood of encouraging messages, a ton of inspirational insights, and some great life lessons.

While working together on our *From the Rafters of Rupp— Legends of Kentucky Basketball* project, I got to know John very well. I learned that not only was he from Lexington, but he also bleeds blue. He grew up a die-hard Kentucky basketball fan. Fifty years later, he's living out his dream covering and writing about something he's knowledgeable and passionate about. You can't fake experience like that. You can't feign the passion.

That's why I know *Kentucky Passion* will be a great success. I'm honored to be a part of it.

Go Cats!

KENTUCKY
PASSION

INTRODUCTION

WHEN IT COMES TO FAN bases in college basketball, nothing matches the passion and fervor of Kentucky's Big Blue Nation. Arguably the largest and most vocal contingent around, the infamous "blue mist" is far-reaching and all-encompassing.

As the program with the most all-time NCAA wins in the history of the sport—including eight national championships, seventeen Final Four appearances, forty-nine SEC regular season championships, thirty-one SEC tournament championships, sixty-three All-Americans and counting—Kentucky fans lay claim to being the "Roman empire" of college basketball. Year after year, the Big Blue faithful return—invigorated and encouraged for another run at glory.

For Wildcat fans worldwide, cheering on their team has become a routine part of life. It's expected, customary, and as natural as breathing air. But citizenship within the Big Blue Nation also carries with it a great sense of privilege and responsibility. Being the guardians over the program with the greatest tradition in the history of college basketball is a mantle Kentucky fans don't take lightly. If truth be told, they're consumed by it. They'll grudgingly admit that their love for their team often surpasses their love for life itself. In other words, *they are passionate about their Cats!*

In *Kentucky Passion*, we take you on a motivational journey inside the Kentucky Basketball dynasty. Through firsthand eye-witness accounts, we'll describe the most defining moments of the Wildcat program and explain how those iconic moments continue to shape the optimism and confidence of Kentucky fans aged eight to eighty. You'll once again relive the night the Goose was golden, you'll reexperience the thrills of the Mardi Gras Miracle, and you'll repeatedly find yourself cheering on the "Unforgettables."

You'll also discover, however, that *Kentucky Passion* is more than just another book about Kentucky Basketball's bygone days of glory. Within this compelling compilation of soul-stirring narratives are valuable life lessons that can change the way you live and think. No longer will these cherished memories be just a pleasant distraction from the rigors of the working world. Now you can actually make them a defining part of your personal life and legacy.

Kentucky Passion provides a year's worth of inspiration. The chapters are designed to be read one per week. Each of the fifty-two chapters begins with an iconic Big Blue moment and concludes with lessons learned and steps moving forward to overcome adversity, strengthen relationships, and bolster confidence within your own sphere of influence. We hope after reading them that you'll be inspired to achieve uncharted levels of personal success while battling through life's most difficult challenges.

So, we encourage you to savor each chapter. Linger over the treasure trove of game-winning shots, heroes of the past, and championship banners. Share them freely with family, friends, neighbors, colleagues at work, or people at church. Mold yourself into the person you were destined to be.

And through it all, be ready to discover how these precious memories—and the collective power of a passionate fan base—can bring home the ultimate victory.

Go Big Blue!

BIG BLUE MADNESS

WEEK 1 | THE MARDI GRAS MIRACLE

ON FEBRUARY 15, 1994, AT around 10:30 p.m., thousands of Kentucky fans turned off their television sets in utter disgust. It was a late Tuesday-night telecast, and the workplace beckoned early the next morning. Plus, the Cats were toast. Coming off losses to Arkansas and Syracuse in the previous two games, Kentucky found themselves in Baton Rouge, trailing LSU 68–37 with less than sixteen minutes left in the contest.

Those who stuck it out were rewarded with one of the greatest comebacks in NCAA history. Those who quit watching couldn't believe their eyes or ears when they learned the next morning about Kentucky's miraculous 99–95 come-from-behind win.

There were a handful of lucky fans who didn't bail out that evening. But they'd be lying if they told you they thought the Cats could still win when they were down big. Kentucky had shown no indication up to that point that they were up to the task. They hadn't won down in the Pete Maravich Assembly Center in nearly six years. On this evening, it looked like that streak would continue as a talented LSU squad seemed to be hitting everything in sight.

Kentucky "only" trailed 48–32 at halftime and had cut the lead to 50–37 when an 18–0 LSU run put the game completely out of reach—or so we thought.

All of a sudden, Kentucky started hitting shots. Walter Mc-Carty, Rodrick Rhodes, and even little-used reserve guard Chris Harrison came off the bench to spark the Wildcats on a 24–4 spurt, cutting the deficit to 72–61 with just under ten minutes to go.

LSU's Ronnie Henderson scored the next five points to extend the lead back out to 16, but Kentucky kept chipping away. Two three-pointers by Jeff Brassow and one each by Rhodes and Travis Ford made it 91–82 with less than 3:30 to play. A minute later, Andre Riddick made a steal and hit Brassow for another trey, and the lead had shrunk to 91–87. The anguished look on LSU coach Dale Brown's face said it all. The Wildcats smelled blood.

Twice, Kentucky traded Clarence Ceasar free throws for three-point buckets. A Tony Delk bomb from the left wing made it 95–93. With thirty seconds left, Delk had the ball again. With the shot clock winding down, he saw McCarty open in the left corner and hit him with the perfect pass. McCarty's high, arcing shot—launched from right in front of the Kentucky bench—nestled gracefully through the nets with only nineteen seconds remaining to give his team a 96–95 lead. The celebration was on for the biggest comeback in UK history!

INSIDE THE HUDDLE

Can you relate to this scenario? Maybe you have a losing streak going in life and feel that some have forgotten about you or even deserted you. This can take a toll on your emotions and make you think you are alone. Perhaps you were laid off and are struggling to find a new job. You might have said some words you regret and hurt someone you love. Maybe because of things you have done in your past, some of your onetime supporters and fans have either left the arena or flipped off the television. Did they lose confidence in you because of your previous performances? Have you lost your self-esteem and think you will never win again? You still have time to put together a run. And, just like the Cats, you can rally for the win.

THE GAME-WINNER

You can make the comeback. Don't ever lose sight of the goal and think the deficit is too massive to overcome. Focus on your strengths and abilities to make the run and put the defense on notice that you have a personal victory in sight. During these tough times, you will find out who you can lean on for inspiration and encouragement. Remember, this is your battle, but you can always use teammates to surround you with love and inspiration.

Give your family and friends a reason to believe in you. If you have a history of losing, put that in the past and go for the win. You can get that offer for a new job. A new relationship might be right around the corner. Expect a good report from your doctor. The point here is to never give up, even when others have walked away. Find those who will support you and get open so they can throw you the ball to hit the game-winning shot.

The Kentucky players could have easily given up, like some of their supporters did. But True Blue fans will stay by your side until the buzzer sounds and the victory has been won. Playing the game is not easy. You might lose some fans, but you will find out who will stick with you through the good and bad times.

Adjustments might be necessary. Maybe you need to apologize to someone or put aside your pride and ask for help. You cannot win alone. You need a team. The victory is always sweeter when you celebrate with others. Be willing to change in order to come out on top. Regain your confidence, and make the run needed to pull out the win and surprise those who thought you were going to lose.

Go Big Blue.

What three adjustments can you make to put yourself in position to win?

_____

_____

_____

_____

_____

_____

_____

_____

_____

_____

_____

_____

_____

_____

_____

_____

_____

_____

_____

_____

_____

_____

_____

_____

WEEK 2 | FOLLOWING A LEGEND

ON MARCH 22, 1985, JOE B. Hall retired after thirteen seasons as the head basketball coach at the University of Kentucky. During that time, the Cynthiana native compiled a gawdy 297–100 record while garnering eight SEC regular season championships, one NIT championship, three NCAA Final Four appearances, and one long-awaited NCAA championship.

While Joe B.'s record speaks for itself, his tenure as Kentucky's head coach could have easily derailed. On March 11, 1978, Hall's heavily favored and number-one-ranked Wildcats found themselves surprisingly trailing Florida State 39–32 at halftime of its NCAA tournament opening-round game in Knoxville. Kentucky fans were in a panic because this was a team expected to win the Cats' first national title in over twenty years.

During the intermission, Joe B. goes ballistic in the locker room over his team's rotten first-half performance, kicking a water bucket as part of his tirade. He then further vents his frustration by benching starters Truman Claytor and All-Americans Jack Givens and Rick Robey in favor of little-used reserves Freddie Cowan, LaVon Williams, and Dwane Casey. Cat fans were beside themselves. *Had Joe lost his mind?* If this move backfired, Joe B. would soon find himself on gamedays selling insurance or hawking timeshares rather than leading from the Kentucky bench.

Fortunately for Joe, the ploy worked to perfection; the quicker, smaller lineup was a much better match against the Seminoles, and the deficit quickly disappeared. As the starters re-entered the game, Kentucky outscored Florida State 53–37 in the second half for a convincing 85–76 victory. The team would then go on to complete the "season without joy" by winning the school's fifth national title.

At this early point in his career, Joe B. Hall was still trying to replace the legendary Adolph Rupp. Make no mistake—it was nearly impossible to replace a legend of Rupp's stature and influence. The "Baron of the Bluegrass" didn't appreciate being forced to step down at the university's mandatory retirement age of seventy. He went out kicking and screaming—aggressively sabotaging many of Hall's efforts to assume command.

"You never want to be the person following the legend," Joe B. once famously said. "You want to be the person following the person following the legend."

He should know. When legendary UCLA head coach John Wooden retired, Joe chimed in by saying that UCLA should have gone ahead and hired him also. "Why ruin two lives," he jokingly quipped.

What many younger fans don't realize is that Joe B. had many detractors within Kentucky's own fan base. When the Wildcats lost to Middle Tennessee State University in the first round of the Mideast regional of the 1982 NCAA tournament, many wanted Joe fired. After all, how could a team with all-stars such as Dirk Minniefield, Jim Master, Charles Hurt, Derrick Hord, Melvin Turpin, and Dicky Beal lose to an opponent with the likes of Ed "Pancakes" Perry and Lucious "Buck" Hailey?

Here's the secret to Joe's eventual success. As the successor to Coach Rupp, Joe B. Hall was "the keeper of the flame." He knew the important role Kentucky Basketball played in the lives of the people of the commonwealth, and he guarded that knowledge with every ounce of his being. He knew how vital it was to keep the fires of passion stoked and the winning tradition alive. From that standpoint, he doesn't get nearly the credit he deserves.

During his coaching tenure, Joe B. took a boatload of All-American prima donnas and not only made them winners on the basketball court but also instilled in them the discipline necessary to be productive young men. That legacy—aided by that comeback victory against Florida State on the way to the 1978 National Championship—would eventually vault him into exalted status as the most beloved coach in the history of the glorious program.

DRAW THE XS AND OS

Many parents long for their children to grow up and become more successful than they themselves were. That is the circle of life. It provides validation to parents.

But it's not always practical. There are two situations here to consider. Maybe you want to push your kids in one direction, but they have a desire to go in another. They might not want to follow in the steps of tradition or follow the pathways you have set for them.

Or you might feel that you haven't lived up to high expectations and have fallen short. Maybe you feel you have let everyone around you down and have not lived up to unreachable prospects.

Expecting others to live up to the plans you have made for them is not fair. This can create bitterness and cause division between family members.

Your dreams that your son or daughter will follow in your footsteps might not be feasible. And, on the other end, dealing with the pressure to live up to the expectations of others can take the wind out of your sails.

CUT DOWN THE NETS

If you are raising children and want to pass down your family heritage, that's fine as long as you can discuss it with them to see if it fits their plans for life. Don't try to force them to be like you; accept them for who they are and can be in life. They are unique, and you must embrace their energy and creativity. If you back off some, you'll give them the space they need to grow and find their own way.

If you're the one who lives with festered disappointments from loved ones because you have chosen to go in a different direction, let go of your guilt and embrace who you are. But always be willing to notice and admit a mistake. Remember the story of the prodigal son?

Communication is the key to any team winning a championship and the key to life. Have conversations and discussions about what you want to do. Don't feel the need to follow in anyone's footsteps unless you want to. And if you wish to blaze your own trail, take it all the way to the hoop for the dunk.

What can you do as a parent to help guide your child in the right direction?

And how can you as a child find your unique path in life?

_____

_____

_____

_____

_____

_____

WEEK 3 | REDEFINING YOUR BRAND

KEITH BOGANS HAS TO BE one of the most underappreciated players in the history of Kentucky Basketball. In 1999, the 6'5" guard—a Parade All-American, a McDonald's All-American, and a *USA Today* All-American out of DeMatha Catholic High School in Maryland—was recruited with high expectations to play for Tubby Smith's Wildcats.

When asked how long he planned to stay at the University of Kentucky, Bogans answered confidently, "One year."

Things didn't work out quite as Keith planned, and that one-and-done year turned into an extended—albeit productive—four-year college career. When he graduated in 2003, Bogans had garnered All-American honors, was the SEC Player of the Year, and had amassed 1,923 total career points, which ranked him fourth on UK's all-time scoring list. Yet many Kentucky fans wouldn't think of mentioning Keith Bogans in such rarefied air.

Many in BBN remember Keith for one thing—his left ankle. On March 23, 2003, number-one-seeded Kentucky was playing Marquette in the finals of the NCAA Midwest regional in Minneapolis. Two nights earlier against Wisconsin, Bogans sustained a severe high ankle sprain. BBN spent the next forty-eight hours in a sustained prayer vigil, hoping that Keith would be able to play. The Cats' twenty-six-game winning streak was obviously in jeopardy.

Keith gutted it out and took the floor, but it was obvious from the get-go that his ankle wasn't 100 percent. Although he scored 14 points in twenty-four minutes of action, his lateral movement was severely limited. Without Bogans's perimeter and transitional game, the Wildcats suddenly became one-dimensional. Combined with a 29-point, 11-rebound, and 11-assist coming-out party by Marquette's Dwyane Wade, Kentucky's dreams of another national championship left the building with the crushing 83–69 upset loss.

At the conclusion of his college career, Keith was selected as the forty-third overall pick in the second round of the 2003 NBA draft by Milwaukee. He ended up playing for nine different NBA teams as basically a role player for most of his twelve-year professional career. Although that was a far cry from his youthful dreams of NBA stardom, you had to give Keith a ton of credit for how well he was able to adapt and adjust.

Not everyone could transition so easily from being the big man on campus to a complementary journeyman coming off a long and talented NBA bench. Keith did just that. He swallowed his pride, worked hard, developed a solid defensive game, and became the consummate teammate in the exclusive play-for-pay league.

How Keith responded to disappointment was a testament to his character. That unfortunate ankle injury most likely cost him a chance at a championship, and his professional career probably wasn't what he had dreamed it would be. But that shouldn't diminish his achievements whatsoever. When additional UK retired jerseys are hoisted up into the rafters of Rupp Arena, Keith Bogans's number 10 should be the next on the list.

THE STARTING LINEUP

This is the moment you have waited for with bated breath. That once-in-a-lifetime job interview. You prepare for days and re-search information on the company; you know you are prepared. You nail it and leave confident your next professional move will be the last. You envision how you will decorate your new corner office and eye that parking space near the entrance. You check your phone over the next few days for that call. Crickets. A week later, your email inbox dings. You were not selected.

Or maybe you have spent several months with the person you want to live the rest of your life with. This is the one, your gut tells you. You imagine where you will go on your honeymoon. But out of nowhere, it ends. You are devasted. Now what?

Or your dream of owning your own business has turned into a nightmare. The confident attitude you once possessed has turned to feelings of failure and disbelief as you watch all those years of hard work go down the drain.

TAPE UP THE ANKLE

Life, just like championships games, is tough to win. It takes hard work and dedication to muster the courage to play through an injury. But if you want to be remembered for being a gutsy player, there is still plenty of time left on the clock. You will twist your ankle in life and face defeats, but that does not mean you give up and become a one-and-out.

Be flexible and willing to adjust your goals in order to raise a banner in your rafters. If you have landed a job you don't en-joy, make the most of it and earn a reputation of being the best employee there.

If you experience a breakup, examine yourself and see if you need to make a halftime adjustment in your personality or attitude.

You might be a journeyman throughout life, and that's okay. Don't let that dampen your ambition. Keep your hopes alive and keep going.

Discouragement can creep into the huddle, but you must recognize when that happens and make the most of any situation. Your attitude and outlook can affect you and those on your team. Just because you are in an undesirable position at the moment does not mean it will always be like that. Look for ways to improve and be patient, but always be ready to make a run to win the game at the right time.

Your brand is at stake. How do you want to be remembered? Go Big Blue.

How can you adjust your expectations and still stay in the hunt to come out a victor? What three things can you do to improve your situation? What needs adjusting in your life?

_____

_____

_____

_____

_____

_____

_____

_____

_____

_____

_____

WEEK 4 | THE NIGHT THE GOOSE WAS GOLDEN

WHEN YOU BANK IN A shot from the corner off the side of the backboard, you know it's going to be your night. That's exactly what happened to Jack "Goose" Givens on the night of March 27, 1978, in the Checkerdome in St. Louis, Missouri. The hometown star from Bryan Station High School capped off an amazing college career with an epic 41-point, 8-rebound performance, propelling the Wildcats to a 94–88 win against the Duke Blue Devils and capturing the school's fifth national title.

Givens, Kentucky's number-three all-time leading scorer with 2,038 total career points, hit 18 of 27 shots from the field that night as 18,721 screaming fans looked on. He scored 16 of Kentucky's final 18 points in the first half as the Wildcats jumped out to a 45–38 lead. His smooth, silky, left-handed jumper consistently found the bottom of the net from the middle of Duke's zone defense. Inexplicably, the Blue Devils never adjusted, and Jack's teammates kept feeding him the ball.

"During the course of the championship game, you're just playing," Givens recounted. "You're just doing what you do and trying your best to do it well. I frankly had no clue as to how many points I had. I knew I was having a good game. I wondered why Duke wasn't changing anything. It was open all night. It wasn't like we were doing anything. It was just the open spot on the floor, and it just so happened that it was my job to fill those open spots."

It was a fitting coronation for a team with four seniors who, as freshmen, advanced to the finals of the 1975 NCAA championship game—only to lose to UCLA in John Wooden's last hurrah. This was an extremely talented and tight-knit team, as evidenced by their 30–2 final season record. But, more importantly, they were uniquely unselfish, with a singular goal in mind. They didn't care who got the glory as long as they won the championship.

With Rick Robey and Mike Phillips serving as twin towers inside, Truman Claytor and Jay Shidler bombing from outside, and Purdue transfer point guard Kyle Macy directing the attack, this group was destined to bring home the hardware.

Super sixth man James Lee's resounding dunk at the buzzer served as a fitting climax for fans who had gone two long decades without experiencing a title. Celebrations erupted across the state, and delirious fans welcomed back the players as conquering heroes returning from battle. The damage to Blue Grass Airport as seven thousand fans flooded in to greet the team—during the wee hours of the morning no less—was widespread, extensive, and costly.

Strains of "Goose" filling the terminal building at 3:30 in the morning were music to so many ears. Later that day in Memorial Coliseum, a crowd of fifteen thousand officially celebrated the victory with an organized pep rally. The first time is often the best time, and for many die-hard Kentucky fans, this 1978 title was the first national championship in their lifetime. It was indeed special.

Givens's performance that evening would later be immortalized in the April 3 *Sports Illustrated* cover and caption: "Goose Was Golden—Givens Leads Kentucky to NCAA Title."

It was an amazing performance by a hometown hero on the biggest stage imaginable. It's an accomplishment that will be difficult to match.

EARLY MORNING WORKOUT SESSION

There is a lost art today, and I don't mean being able to bank a shot off the glass from the corner. Although that is spectacular when it happens, any shooter will tell you that is not their intent. If they tried to bank from that angle, they would be unsuccessful 90 percent of the time. But the key point here is to put yourself in position for that to happen. Take enough shots in life, and you will pull it off. But you cannot do it alone, even though you are the one who launched it from the corner. You have to have help and a supporting cast. And you must play together and depend on one another to be victorious. There is one key element when it comes to winning in life.

IT'S GAME TIME

The lost art I spoke about earlier is humility. It's an admirable trait that goes unnoticed and unpromoted today. Players on the 1978 team had a singular goal in mind, and that was overall team success. They did not care who received the headlines or the glory as long as they won in the end. No matter what it took, the ultimate goal was a banner.

Now, this does not mean to win at all costs. It means putting others first and helping one another during the two halves of life.

Instead of knocking a coworker off a pedestal, lift them up and help them to receive recognition.

Instead of complaining that a person is taking too long in line at a restaurant, pay for the meal of the person behind you, but don't tell them. It's about having perspective and thinking of others.

Volunteer your time with a civic organization and reach down to help someone in need. Humility and teamwork are the goal—and you will benefit from the emotions pitted deep within the heart of a champion.

Forgo the hoopla and fanfare. You can do without the pats on the back, even though those can be nice and validating at times. Do something because you want to win and not for the glory and recognition.

Get up on a crisp Saturday morning and cancel the tee time. Invite your friends out for a cup of coffee and encourage them to go with you to a soup kitchen and give your time to help someone else.

Humility. Service. Unselfishness.

That is what winners are made of. Go Big Blue.

How can you be more of a team player? List some ways you can turn off the limelight and turn your attention to others.

_____

_____

_____

_____

_____

_____

_____

_____

_____

_____

_____

WEEK 5 | RISE OF THE "JORTS"

IF YOU'RE LOOKING FOR A "rags to riches" story, look no further than Josh Harrellson. The 6'10" center, who began his UK career in 2008 as an unheralded transfer from Southwestern Illinois Junior College, was best known by Kentucky fans for one particular wardrobe item—jean shorts.

"Jorts"—as he was affectionately known—played initially under Coach Billy Gillispie. His greatest claim to fame during that time occurred during a road game against the Vanderbilt Commodores in 2009. Harrellson wasn't performing up to Coach Gillispie's standards and subsequently found himself banished to the restroom toilet stall as punishment. He was also later "encouraged" to ride in the team's equipment van by himself on the way back to Lexington.

Things didn't improve much the next season. Gillispie was gone by then, and John Calipari was the new sheriff in town. He didn't take kindly to Harrellson's lackadaisical attitude or work ethic. When Josh put out a cryptic tweet about his new coach, everyone thought his UK career was on life support.

But suddenly, things changed. In a matter of weeks, Cat fans saw a brand-new Josh Harrellson. He got into fabulous shape, worked hard in practice, and developed a new mindset. By the latter part of the 2010–2011 season, he had rightfully earned the full confidence of his teammates and coaches.

With Turkish all-star recruit Enes Kanter not cleared by the NCAA to play that season, Harrellson was pressed into action. He scored 289 total points—shooting over 61 percent from the field—and grabbed 329 rebounds over the course of his thirty-eight games. His one shining moment happened on March 25, 2011, in the first half of the Wildcats' Sweet Sixteen East regional showdown against top-ranked Ohio State.

The Buckeyes were led by Jared Sullinger, a consensus All-American and Wooden Award finalist. Sullinger was a brute of a player, terrorizing his opponents down low with his strength and agility. Harrellson held his own, however. He played physical defense on Sullinger for the entire game on his way to an impressive 17-point, 10-rebound performance.

With three and a half minutes to go in the first half and Kentucky trailing 27–25, Harrellson went for a rebound and appeared to be pushed by Sullinger. As he was stumbling out of bounds, Harrellson turned and rocketed the ball off of Sullinger's chest. It was a move worthy of the Dodgeball Hall of Fame and showed the entire world that "Jorts" would not be intimidated.

After a thrilling 62–60 upset victory over the Buckeyes on a game-winning jumper by Brandon Knight, Kentucky went on in the next game to defeat North Carolina in the regional finals for another trip to the Final Four.

Harrellson's March Madness performance up to that point, where he averaged 14.8 points and 9 rebounds, undoubtedly made him ponder a potential NBA future.

"It makes me happy because I may have a career after Kentucky now," he said immediately after the season concluded. "That's what I am going to be focusing on now."

Josh "Jorts" Harrellson was selected number forty-five overall in the second round of the 2011 NBA draft by the New Orleans Hornets. He played three seasons in the NBA, supplemented by a highly successful professional career overseas.

Not bad for a guy who Coach Cal almost kicked off the team.

THE PEP RALLY

What first impression do you make? Does your boss admire your attitude? Do you inspire your friends? What does the way you dress say to those around you?

You often get one opportunity for people to judge your character, and your appearance plays a role in influencing your reputation.

To receive a nickname based on your normal attire might be a little daunting. Your attitude and outlook say a lot about you and send a message to others about whether or not you care.

While your favorite T-shirt and sweatpants might be comfortable to wear in the office, if you're meeting clients for lunch, this will not fly.

Living up to the standards and expectations of your employers, colleagues, friends, and family is important. Accountability and responsibility are vital to your success.

HALFTIME ADJUSTMENTS

Everyone gets in a rut and needs encouragement sometimes. But when it's crunch time, you need to snap out of it and take control of some areas in your life.

Attitude is one of them.

The one "Jorts" displayed nearly got him kicked off one of the most prestigious programs in college sports. His lackluster outlook was not one to be admired.

If your boss has a dress code, honor it. Athletes wear the uniform and adhere to the rules. Rebellion will bring a technical foul or lead to being thrown off the court.

If those who care about you tell you that your attitude needs an adjustment, take that into consideration. Put the ego aside and make some changes.

The first thing you need to do is understand what changes are needed. Take an honest and in-depth inventory of yourself. If you are negative all the time, start focusing on the positive. Find the good in every situation.

Consider searching for a mentor or role model. This might be someone who has many years of service to your company and knows the ropes of true success, or maybe it's a pastor or Sunday school teacher. Learning from those who have done well is a good start.

Your outlook will affect your life. Set goals and work hard to achieve them. When you get hit, get back up and find a way to use that experience to learn a life lesson. Always take responsibility for your actions and strive to do better.

Sometimes the company you keep can drag you down as well. Take an inventory of those around you and consider whether you need to make new friends. Bad community corrupts good character, and misery loves company. Find companions who will support you, lift you up, and challenge you to do the right thing.

And, finally, have confidence in yourself, but don't allow cockiness to creep in. There is a difference.

Go Cats.

How can you change your attitude?

WEEK 6 | THE "SKY'S" THE LIMIT

ASK ANY KENTUCKY FAN WHO was alive in the 1980s what they remember about Charles Barkley and they'll all tell you the same thing: they remember the "Round Mound of Rebound" sitting on the basketball court bawling his eyes out after Kentucky defeated Auburn 51–49 in the 1984 SEC tournament in Nashville.

The date was March 10, 1984, to be exact. Third-ranked Kentucky—loaded with the likes of Sam Bowie, Melvin Turpin, Jim Master, Dicky Beal, Winston Bennett, James Blackmon, Bret Bearup, and Kenny Walker—was facing an unranked Auburn squad within the confines of Memorial Gymnasium in Music City. The game went back and forth—a tight defensive slugfest resulting in a 49–49 tie as the final seconds ticked off the clock. When Kenny Walker's last-second shot "doinked" into the basket to give Kentucky the win, Barkley sat despondently on the court, visibly shaken over the final outcome.

"With about eight seconds to go, Coach Hall calls a timeout," Walker recalled. "My eyes got really big because I couldn't believe he was actually drawing up a play for me. I come off a pick and catch the ball with about two seconds to go. I had enough time to elevate, but I must admit it wasn't the prettiest shot in the world. It was a line drive, hit the front of the rim, bounced up about two feet over the rim, and swished back through with no time on the clock."

"As time expired, the camera pans to Charles Barkley," Kenny continued, "and he's crying on the floor. A lot of fans call in on my radio show and talk about that moment. They always say, 'Kenny, you're the only guy to make Charles Barkley cry.'"

Kenny "Sky" Walker grew up in Roberta, Georgia, a tiny town of about a thousand people. He confesses it was hard leaving home and going away to college. Kenny was painfully shy, and playing in front of twenty-three thousand rabid, screaming fans in Lexington, Kentucky, was a huge adjustment at first. But his four years under the microscope would most assuredly serve him well later in life.

Walker, Kentucky's number-two all-time leading scorer with 2,080 total career points, was drafted number five overall in the first round of the 1986 NBA draft by the New York Knicks. For the next five seasons, "Sky" would experience, firsthand, all the glitz and glamour of playing under the bright lights on the big stage of the Big Apple.

After a successful professional career, which included winning the 1989 NBA slam dunk contest, Kenny returned to Lexington, where he now serves as the ultimate ambassador for Big Blue Nation. He's always good for a friendly wave, an impromptu chat, and a quick "hello" with adoring fans. Regardless of circumstances or setting, you'll never see him turn down an autograph request or multiple selfies.

"Today, I'm a living witness of all the things that have happened in my life—before Kentucky and after UK," Walker admits. "I'd say that decision [to attend the University of Kentucky] changed my life forever because of the rapport that I have with the fans and the people that I've met throughout my career. That's the most important thing to me."

That and the fact that he made Charles Barkley cry.

IN THE FILM ROOM

You have studied your opponent for days and feel confident you know the team's strengths and weaknesses. Now it's game time, and you feel a bit uneasy and nervous. That's normal. If you didn't have a queasy feeling inside before a major event or decision, there might be something wrong.

You will be faced with some major choices in life. You might land that job of a lifetime, but it involves moving away from everything you know and love. Or maybe it's the opposite, and you have a desire to break away and make a fresh start.

Don't ever run away; instead go forward with a positive mindset. Sometimes you just have to trust your gut instincts, and it never hurts to look to God for comfort.

TAKE THE SHOT

The last thing you want to reflect on is the chance you never took. A regret may haunt you and hold you down for years into the future.

Maybe it's that chance to open your own business or to ask for a job interview. Or it could be something small that you've always wanted to do. The point here is to take a chance. But don't do it on a whim and without a plan.

When you take a chance, you will discover who you are. When you toss yourself into the unknown, you may be getting out of an environment that is holding you back. Find out who you are and what you want to do and put yourself in position to take the shot and define your character and attitude.

When you take a chance, you will have an attitude of rejuvenation and a desire to prove something to yourself. But never do this out of rebellion or revenge. Taking a chance can be fun, but there might also be stumbling blocks. Be ready for success and some failure along the way.

Use fear to motivate you when you start something new. Being afraid is okay, but don't let it define who you are. Remember the anxiety you had the first time you rode a roller coaster? When the ride ended, you either hated it or wanted to ride again. But in both cases, you conquered the emotion.

Taking chances will give you a sense of freedom. It's fine to depend on friends and loved ones for encouragement and stability, but the day may come when you want to take a chance because you know it's right. Be ready for a debate from those who love you and support from others. Weigh the options and put yourself in a position to take that shot in the end. You might stumble and clank it off the backboard, but then again—just like Kenny "Sky" Walker—you might just ease it over the rim to win the championship. You won't know unless you shoot the ball.

Make sure your expectations are realistic, but also keep your eyes on that special trophy. Have confidence in yourself, and don't be afraid to take that leap of faith.

Remember, the sky is the limit.

Go Big Blue.

What can you do to prepare yourself for that moment?

_____

_____

_____

_____

_____

_____

_____

WEEK 7 | "UNFORGETTABLE" MOMENTS

"KENTUCKY'S SHAME." FOR WILDCAT FANS worldwide, that was the *Sports Illustrated* cover article that signaled the end of the Roman empire of college basketball. May 29, 1989—a day that will live in infamy. Cash to a player in the mysterious Emery Freight envelope and allegations of cheating on a college entrance exam put the vaunted Kentucky program on NCAA probation for three interminable years. Throw in some scholarship limits and a ban on postseason play, and you could easily understand why fans were despondent and discouraged.

Through the turmoil of the investigation and the search for a new coach, four selfless players decided to stick it out. Richie Farmer (Clay County), Deron Feldhaus (Maysville), John Pelphrey (Paintsville), and Sean Woods (Indianapolis) took a fan base on life support and readied the downtrodden for a nearly immaculate resurrection.

Under the guidance of first-year coach Rick Pitino, these four homegrown heroes hustled their way to an improbable 14–14 record—with a team so devoid of talent that many predicted they would be lucky to win four games. Along the way, they slew Goliath—in the form of a twelfth-ranked LSU team with a roster stacked with the likes of Shaquille O'Neal, Chris Jackson, and Stanley Roberts. On February 15, 1990, before 24,301 delirious fans in a cacophonous Rupp Arena, the Cats somehow prevailed, setting the stage for arguably the most iconic moment in Kentucky Basketball lore.

After an amazing 22–6 campaign the following year, the sanctions were finally lifted for the 1991–1992 season. On Saturday, March 28, the Cats found themselves in the Spectrum in Philadelphia, playing against a top-ranked Duke team in the NCAA East regional final. By this time, sixth-ranked Kentucky was no chopped liver either. Anchored by 6'8" superstar forward Jamal "Monster Mash" Mashburn, this group of overachieving role players had Kentucky in the hunt for another national championship—miraculously just three years short of the program's nadir.

The game, described by many—including Bob Ryan of the *Boston Globe*—as the "best game ever," had it all. Full-court action, sudden lead changes, improbable athletic feats, and the villainous stomp by Christian Laettner onto the chest of a prone and defenseless Aminu Timberlake—it was drama that even Hollywood couldn't fabricate.

When Sean Woods hit the greatest "soon to be forgotten" shot in UK history, Kentucky was up 103–102 with only 2.1 seconds left in overtime. The Big Blue faithful in the house, together with the multitudes glued to their television sets back home, could finally taste another long-awaited trip to the Final Four. A fairy-tale ending was just one defensive stop away.

Occasionally, however, even fairy tales end badly. By now you know exactly what happened next. Those brutal and relentless CBS Sports March Madness promotional videos won't let you ever forget. That three-quarters of the court, unguarded inbounds pass from Grant Hill to Christian Laettner is what True Blue nightmares are made of. Laettner's "shot" subsequently pierced the collective hearts of those looking on in disbelief, sending grown men into spasms of despair. Duke 104–Kentucky 103.

Surprisingly for most, the sun did rise the very next day. Fans quickly realized the magnitude of what had just transpired. A once proud Kentucky program, mired in ashes, had risen back to its exalted place of honor among the blue-blooded elite. When UK athletics director C. M. Newton unveiled their jerseys shortly afterward in the hallowed rafters of Rupp Arena, these four "unforgettable" greats became permanently sealed in the beating hearts of an adoring Big Blue Nation.

THE 5:00 A.M. WORKOUT

Do you feel alone? Did you wake up one day to find that people you thought supported you were nowhere to be found? Maybe you believe you are an underdog with little chance of winning.

You feel abandoned, and life is throwing sanctions at you that will not allow you to have a shot at winning.

Maybe you have gone through a job loss or a major personal breakdown. Perhaps illness has stolen valuable time from you and left you to fend for yourself.

In times of trial and discouragement, perhaps some on your "team" have left town to join other programs.

You look around, and only a few people remain on the court. But really, that's all you need.

MAKE THE ROSTER

No one needs fair-weather fans—neither in athletics nor in real life.

Character is built under pressure, and determination is a key to reaping rewards.

Will you face failure and adversity? Of course. But along the way, you will discover something admirable deep inside of you.

The easy way out is to quit or to move on to another situation.

But a sense of accomplishment will only come if you persevere and see your mission through to the end. The results might not be immediate, but they may appear in the fourth quarter.

There are ways to stay motivated and focused instead of quitting. Even when others walk away from you, seek inspiration to keep fighting for what you believe is right.

Set a defined goal and put your ideas into action. Create a clear vision that will allow you to see the big picture. A game plan is essential to produce a win in the end.

The hardest thing to do during tough times is to maintain a positive attitude, but it's a must. You can accomplish this by breaking your goals down into manageable tasks to increase your odds of hitting them.

Get organized and develop a game plan and that does not include procrastination. Don't be fooled by the full-court press of life and set deadlines that are impossible to hit.

Believe in your heart that hard work does pay off in the end and that a strong work ethic still has meaning.

If most of your teammates have bolted for another opportunity and left you trailing at halftime, dig down and find a few who still believe in you and will go into overtime with you to make sure you win.

Go Big Blue.

What obstacles do you face, and what plan can you make to overcome them? How can you make some unforgettable moments?

_____

_____

_____

_____

_____

WEEK 8 | THE GREATEST STORY EVER TOLD

"IT'S FRUSTRATING WHEN YOU LOSE. But coming up, we know what we can do. It's going to be a great story."

Those were the prophetic words uttered on March 1, 2014, by Kentucky guard Aaron Harrison in the postgame interview room after a demoralizing 72–67 road loss to the South Carolina Gamecocks. It appeared that the Wildcats' once-promising season had run completely off the rails. Kentucky, clinging to a number-seventeen national ranking, had lost two out of three and were in the midst of a late-winter slide.

Watching this game was like pulling teeth. Against a struggling Carolina team that had only won five games all season, the Cats at one point missed 14 straight shots and wound up shooting 27 percent from the field. To add insult to injury, Coach John Calipari was ejected midway through the second half after picking up his second technical foul. Although Kentucky made a valiant comeback—cutting a 16-point deficit to 1—it just wasn't enough. As if to rub it in, the South Carolina student body stormed the court of Colonial Life Arena when the final horn sounded.

By this point in the season, with the inexplicable losses rising, many in BBN were ready to throw in the towel. Little did they know that Aaron and the Wildcats were preparing for their greatest run ever.

Kentucky would finish the regular season at 22–9 (12–6 in the SEC) with another 85–64 blowout loss at Florida. They would then lose to the Gators again, 61–60, in the championship game of the SEC tournament in Atlanta. When March Madness finally arrived, the window for redemption had rapidly closed.

After a rather pedestrian 56–49 first-round NCAA tournament win over a pesky Kansas State team in St. Louis, the unimaginable happened. Kentucky went on a four-game run that remains to this day, for many Kentucky fans, the most exciting moment they've ever experienced in sports—*period!*

Think about it. Four nail-biting NCAA tournament victories against four top-caliber teams (78–76 over Wichita State in St. Louis, 74–69 over archrival Louisville and 75–72 over Michigan in the Midwest regionals in Indianapolis, and 74–73 over Wisconsin in the national semifinals in Dallas) on the biggest stage in collegiate sports—all essentially settled by a clutch Aaron Harrison three-pointer as the game winds down. One of these moments is enough to send you through the roof. Four consecutive games sends you into orbit.

When Aaron Harrison launched his shot with seven seconds to go and Kentucky down by two to Wisconsin in the national semifinal game, Jim Nance of CBS Sports said on the broadcast, "This is the point where he always hits it."

Hit it he did, sending all of BBN into a euphoria that may never be matched. Afterward, frenzied UK fans were delirious—as if they had a bolus of adrenaline injected directly into their pulsating veins. Cat fans everywhere were in their happy place, ecstatic on cloud nine.

Two nights later, Kentucky would lose to UConn 60–54 in the national championship game. But I'll say it again—immediately after the South Carolina loss, Aaron Harrison knew what was coming. That four-game run into the Final Four by the 2014 Wildcats remains the greatest Kentucky Basketball story ever told.

LATE-NIGHT FILM SESSION

What has discouraged you and dampened your fire to succeed? You might have had a big bruiser slam dunk on you and then stand over you and beat their chest. What dark moments have you faced?

Maybe you were fired from your dream job, and the bills are due. Perhaps you received depressing news from your doctor that punched you in the gut and caught you off guard.

Life is not fair sometimes. You will face dark days. No one likes to talk about it, but circumstances and situations can present themselves at what seems to be the worst times.

Maybe your spouse has left you, or a conflict with a child has led them astray.

Or perhaps you poured your heart and soul into making your business a success, but the pandemic sent it tumbling into failure.

OVERTIME

The Wildcats could have taken the easy route by tossing in the towel and accepting defeat.

Legendary women's basketball coach Pat Summitt once said, "Winning is fun . . . sure. But winning is not the point. Wanting to win is the point. Not giving up is the point. Never letting up is the point. Never being satisfied with what you've done is the point."

We become discouraged when our expectations and reality conflict with each other. Many times, your expectations might seem too high to reach. The reality is that most things that are worthwhile take a lot of effort and time to make happen. Be patient.

Also know that you can replace failure with education. Learn from the loss. Let it motivate you. Don't deny it happened, but use it to gain experience and inspiration so it doesn't happen again the next time.

You can choose to let it define you, or you can look at it as an opportunity to grow your knowledge base.

In any case, stay true to your goals and visions, and strategize ways to rebound from the loss.

Capitalize on your next chance to play and go for the win.

Another aspect to remember is to remain humble. A bruised ego is often the real reason you are discouraged and defeated. Take control of your attitude and effort and use these tools to get back into the game.

When you are strong enough to listen to criticism and suggestions from mentors, pastors, or friends, this allows opportunities for positive personal and spiritual growth.

Before you know it, you will find the grit and determination you need to overcome past discouragement.

Put yourself in a position to live the greatest story ever told. Be the example. Go Big Blue!

How did your dark days make you stronger?

What lessons did you learn?

WEEK 9 | BE LIKE KYLE

IF YOU WERE A BOY (or girl) born during or shortly after Kentucky's 1978 championship run, there's a pretty good chance your name is Kyle. That's Kyle for Kyle Macy, arguably the most popular player to ever wear the Blue and White. Considering the ungodly amount of basketball talent that has flowed through Lexington over the years, that's saying a lot.

Macy, the transfer point guard from Purdue, was just what the doctor ordered for the '78 Wildcats. At 6'3"—with perfectly coiffed hair and dark brown eyes—he could make women swoon. He wasn't necessarily the fastest, strongest, or quickest guard on the floor, but he was as pure a point guard as you could ask for. Macy was smart and unselfish, could pass the ball, and had a really pure stroke from the outside. Most importantly, he made all his teammates better. And, boy, could he shoot free throws.

While at the charity stripe, Kyle developed a ritual where he would bend down and wipe his hands on his socks before he was handed the ball to shoot. Because Kyle Macy did it, every kid shooting hoops in Kentucky started doing the very same thing. Simply put, back then everybody in the commonwealth wanted to be like Kyle.

The toughest game for that 1978 team on their way to the championship occurred on March 18 in Dayton, Ohio.

Number-one-ranked Kentucky was playing number-four-ranked Michigan State in the Mideast regional finals for the right to advance to the Final Four. The Spartans, led by Magic Johnson and Greg Kelser, shot 57 percent from the floor in the first half, jumping out to a 27–22 halftime lead.

The second half saw Michigan State stretch the lead to 31–24 before Kentucky made its run. At the suggestion of assistant coach Leonard Hamilton, Coach Joe B. Hall instructed Macy and senior forward Rick Robey to start playing a pick-and-roll game.

"I'd read off the pick and get in the gap and try to hit Jack [Givens] on the wing or Rick rolling back," was the way Macy explained it. "As it worked out, they backed off of me, and I got a few shots to go and got a few fouls when they were late getting to me. And I was fortunate enough to hit the shots."

Hit them he did. For the game, Macy—who played the entire forty minutes—was 10 for 11 from the foul line and led the team with 18 total points as Kentucky squeaked by with a 52–49 win. Macy scored 7 of Kentucky's final 9 points, all of them clutch free throws from the foul stripe.

As talented as that 1978 squad was, there's no way they get by Michigan State without Kyle Macy. You know it, BBN knows it, and a lot of middle-aged Kyles born in Kentucky know it.

CALL FOR THE HUDDLE

Now more than ever, great leaders and role models are needed to set the example for today's generation. Throughout history, leaders have been admired and even feared to some extent.

Fathers and mothers were respected, and elders were revered for their wisdom and experience. Decisions were final, and the time-out generation did not exist.

The family has become a dwindling institution and needs to be restored. Families need leaders, both men and women, who will stand up for their values, morals, and convictions.

Maybe you have been thrust into a leadership role. Perhaps you inherited it by being born as the eldest brother or sister, and your siblings look to you for answers.

Or perhaps you are a first-time parent, and you now have a responsibility to raise your child up in the way you think is best.

Do you want someone else to set the example for your child? No. You must step up to the line, wipe your socks, and nail the free throws.

THE PICK-N-ROLL

Leaders are often revealed during times of pressure. Whether it's in the boardroom, classroom, or family room, you can rise to the top.

Children respect someone who takes charge and sets boundaries. As a parent, your responsibility is not to be their best friend but to be someone who guides them in the right direction. It's not easy, but you must deliver.

Be strong but courteous. Shouting out orders does not make you a leader.

Show kindness without weakness. When you demonstrate a kind heart and attitude, you show strength. Consider all angles and points of view, and don't concede your beliefs.

You can be bold without being a bully. You should never push your ideals on others, but should be prepared to offer a logical explanation as to why you hold to certain standards. Communication is key.

Show humility, and let others see your compassion for those in need and how you put your own desires last. Lift up those who are down and lend a hand. Make time for those close to you, and don't focus on grabbing the spotlight for a job well done.

Laugh often, especially at yourself. When you can distinguish yourself as being witty and fun, as opposed to being silly and foolish, those around you will feel at ease. But make sure you get the job done and make time for others around you.

You can be a leader. You can be the one your family and friends turn to when the game is on the line. Step up, take a deep breath, focus on the task, wipe your socks, get a good vision of success, and listen for the swoosh of the net after the ball goes through the hoop.

Be a leader. Be the consummate point guard. Be like Kyle.

What characteristics of being a good leader do you feel fit your personality? How can you lead your family or friends?

_____

_____

_____

_____

_____

_____

_____

_____

_____

_____

_____

_____

_____

WEEK 10 | THIS IS MY STAGE

MANY CAT FANS WOULD TELL you that Anthony Davis was the greatest and most impactful player to ever wear the Wildcat uniform. I know that's a very strong and direct statement, but there's plenty of evidence to back it up. The truth is that Davis achieved more in his one year at Kentucky than other uber-talented players have accomplished in their two-, three-, or four-year careers.

In the 2011–2012 season, Davis—a 6'10" Chicago native—was the National Player of the Year, the National Defensive Player of the Year, the National Freshman of the Year, the NCAA Final Four Most Outstanding Player, a consensus First Team All-American, a First Team All-SEC selection, the SEC Player of the Year, the SEC Defensive Player of the Year, the SEC Freshman of the Year, and a member of the All-SEC Freshman team, the All-SEC Tournament team, and the All-NCAA Regional team. Throw in an NCAA championship, an Olympic gold medal, and becoming the number-one overall pick in the 2012 NBA draft, and you can easily see why many would proclaim him the GOAT.

In the 2012 NCAA semifinals in the Superdome in New Orleans, immediately after Kentucky's 69–61 win over in-state rival Louisville, Davis shared his now famous "this is my stage" victory celebration with the rest of the college basketball world. After his dominating 18-point, 14-rebound, 5-block performance in the first ever Final Four clash between the two marquee programs, who could blame him?

Even Louisville's head coach, Rick Pitino—not one to ever shun hyperbole—seemed sincerely impressed with how Davis played.

"Anthony Davis is just the number-one player in the draft," he said of the nineteen-year-old phenom. "When you're playing against Bill Russell on the pro level, you realize why the Celtics won eleven world championships."

Two nights later, on April 2, in the championship game against Kansas, Davis and his unibrow were just as dominant. The fact that he shot 1 for 10 from the field and only scored 6 total points didn't really matter. His 16 rebounds, 6 blocked shots, 5 assists, 3 steals, and general court presence still garnered him the game's MVP trophy and the 67–59 UK victory.

It's been well documented how much confidence the selfless Davis had in the rest of his teammates that night.

"Well, it's not me, it's these guys behind me," he explained. "They led us this whole tournament. This whole game, I was struggling offensively, and I told my team, every time down, you all score the ball. I'm just gonna defend and rebound."

Although this Kentucky team had plenty of NBA talent to go around, Davis was *the* vital cog in securing John Calipari's first NCAA championship and Kentucky's eighth national title.

Under the brightest lights of college basketball, Anthony Davis excelled on his biggest stage.

THE PREGAME INTERVIEW

Do you feel you have an abundance of talent but have not been on the stage to prove yourself to others? Maybe you feel like you are a diamond in the rough, just waiting on your chance to shine.

Waiting for that moment can be excruciating.

Maybe you have a great education, but you struggle to find a sustainable occupation. Perhaps you are ready to settle down with someone special, but you can't find the right person.

Expect your day in the spotlight to come. You may grow weary of hearing this but be encouraged that hard work and patience pay off in the end.

You need to believe that one day you will burst on to the scene and capture the title. It might not come exactly like it did for Anthony Davis, but you will cut down the nets.

GRAB THE SPOTLIGHT

When your day in the sun arrives, face it with humility and gratitude. No one likes a boastful winner.

When you begin to grow into a journey that appears to be reaching the big stage, don't lose sight of those individuals who helped you on the way up.

Keep your dreams in sight and chase them. Find your true calling, whether it is something that grabs the headlines or involves working behind the scenes.

When you pursue your ambitions, be determined to see your goals through to the end.

Will there be applause and accolades? Who knows? Does it matter? This should not be your focus. Be ready to share the spotlight with all who are involved in helping you climb the ladder to reach this achievement. You should always share the credit and the praise.

Always sustain your motivation, even in times of discouragement. When you have an overall goal in sight, you should expect setbacks. But don't let them stop you from reaching your desired target. And when you win the game, you will enjoy it all the more.

When the time does come and you stand on that bright stage, accept the recognition with class and sportsmanship.

My son's high school baseball coach told his players when you hit your first home run, run around the bases like you've done it two dozen times.

No one likes cockiness or arrogance. Never rub your success in the face of your opponents, even if they do that to you. Win with class and humility and accept temporary defeat with dignity.

You are practicing for the big dance every day. Make sure you stretch and get loose and execute the game plan. Depend on your teammates to pick up the load when you struggle, and always give credit when it's due to others.

How can you play on the big stage? Who has helped you find success? How can you show gratitude?

_____

_____

_____

_____

_____

_____

_____

_____

_____

_____

_____

_____

WEEK 11 | CHARITY BEGINS WITH CAL

KENTUCKY HEAD COACH JOHN CALIPARI remains one of the most polarizing figures in the basketball world. His supporters think he walks on water. His detractors regard him as the Antichrist. Whether you're a fan of the one-and-done—or even if you have a disdain for vacated national titles—one thing remains crystal clear: Coach Cal's heart beats with genuine compassion when dealing with those in need.

Coaching basketball at Kentucky is about more than just diagramming Xs and Os. Sure, winning games is important, but that's often outweighed by responsibilities off the court. In Coach Cal's mind, winning a national title often seems secondary to teaching his players about love, largesse, and life. Not surprisingly, that philosophy irks many fans.

Calipari's record on the court is impressive, but his charitable actions off the hardwood are even more admirable. While coaching the Memphis Tigers, Calipari was a big supporter of Streets Ministries, a Christian-based organization that helps inner-city youth. When he left Memphis for UK in 2009, he pledged an additional million dollars to that charitable operation. That's putting your money where your mouth is.

Calipari's altruism and benevolence continued when he arrived in Lexington. During his first season, a devastating earthquake struck the island nation of Haiti. Coach Cal and his 2009–2010 team conducted a telethon, raising more than $1.3 million for the earthquake victims. Whether helping at a tornado relief fundraiser for the local citizens of West Liberty, conducting a disaster relief telethon for Hurricane Harvey casualties, or raising money for federal workers during the 2019 government shutdown, Coach Cal's generous spirit seems ubiquitously free flowing.

At no time was that more evident than when Calipari took his team to the Bahamas for the 2018 preseason. Samaritan's Feet is a humanitarian aid organization that shares a message of hope and love through washing the feet of impoverished children around the world and providing them with new shoes. The day prior to their first exhibition game, the UK players, Coach Cal, and the UK staff partnered with the nonprofit charity to visibly spread God's message.

"When the kids come, you can tell, you know, they don't have much," Coach Cal explained to his players. "They have a pair of shoes for them, but before they give them the shoes, you wash their feet. Do you know the connotation of that? Washing their feet? Why would you wash their feet? It shows servant leadership. Who washed the feet of the twelve disciples? That's what Jesus did. He washed their feet."

But that's not all. Never one to duck away from social issues, Calipari recently spearheaded the John McLendon Minority Leadership Initiative, a coordinated effort to help minorities gain access to jobs in athletics administration. And, of course, there's also the Calipari Foundation, whose mission is to "provide for the physical, educational, and developmental needs of people and communities, while encouraging and equipping others to do the same." The charity's reach is far and wide within the Lexington community, and many of its initiatives go completely unpublicized.

"King Rex" Chapman does the "Y" during a time-out at Rupp Arena.
All photo credits: Dr. Michael Huang

De'Aaron Fox schools Lonzo Ball in the 2017
NCAA tournament in Memphis.

Shai Gilgeous-Alexander surpasses his five-star teammates
in a surprise one-and-done season.

De'Aaron Fox was just one of many first-round NBA draft
picks to come out of the University of Kentucky.

Confetti rains down on the Superdome in New Orleans as
the Wildcats win championship number eight in 2012.

University of Kentucky president Eli Capilouto presents head coach
John Calipari with the 2012 NCAA championship trophy.

Anthony Davis displays one of his signature blocks during
the 2012 NCAA championship game versus Kansas.

Derek Anderson's ACL injury in 1997 might have cost the Wildcats a national championship and a three-peat.

Kenny "Sky" Walker remains arguably the ultimate goodwill ambassador for the Big Blue Nation.

Malik Monk, another one of John Calipari's first-round
NBA draft selections, soars for an acrobatic dunk.

The University of Kentucky Cheerleaders, winner of a record twenty-four national championships, interacts with the crowd at Rupp Arena.

John Calipari presents his annual "state of the union" manifesto at Kentucky's Big Blue Madness tip-off to the season.

Former All-Americans Kyle Macy and Jack "Goose"
Givens from Kentucky's 1978 national championship team
greet fellow All-American great and former UK athletics
director Cliff Hagan at a recent reunion event.

Former All-American and "Fiddlin' Five" member Vernon Hatton chats with John Calipari (probably about his forty-seven-foot shot against the Temple Owls on December 7, 1957—a date that will *not* live in infamy).

Left to right: Jeff Sheppard, "Wah Wah" Jones, Derek Anderson, Cliff Hagan, Ron Mercer, Joe B. Hall, Adrian Smith, Vernon Hatton, Jack Givens, and Kyle Macy hoist another championship banner.

Tyler Ulis gives his bloody-eyed stare-down to the Louisville Cardinals in the Wildcats' 2014–2015 Armageddon showdown with little brother.

UCLA cries "mercy" as Aaron Harrison and the Cats
complete a 41–7 first-half beatdown of the mighty Bruins
in the 2014 CBS Sports Classic in Chicago.

Devin Booker, Tyler Ulis, Trey Lyles, and Willie Cauley-Stein enjoy the carnage left over from another Kentucky blowout victory in the 2014–2015 undefeated regular season.

DeMarcus "Boogie" Cousins goes in for another monster jam. Call me?

A couple of decades after getting his chest stomped on, Aminu
Timberlake (together with all of BBN) still "hates Christian Laettner."

The ESPN crew of Rece Davis, Jay Williams, Digger Phelps, and Jay Bilas at one of many GameDay appearances at Rupp Arena.

Josh "Jorts" Harrellson stuffs Ohio State's Jared Sullinger
in their 2011 East regional Sweet Sixteen showdown.

Josh Harrellson slams home 2 of his 17 points in Kentucky's 2011 upset thriller over Ohio State in the Wildcats' march toward another Final Four.

Brandon Knight drills a last-second jumper over Ohio State's Aaron Craft
to give Kentucky a 62–60 upset win over the top-ranked Buckeyes.

"Traitor Rick" Pitino exchanges pregame pleasantries with
John Calipari prior to suffering another brutal beatdown.

So why does he do all this when he could just sit back and coach his team? Coach Cal credits his late mother, Donna, for much of his philanthropic inspiration.

"My mother taught me to pay it forward," he said of the good fortune that comes around to certain people. "That was her mantra, and I've never forgotten it. If I see someone who needs help, I know I can't save the world. But if there is something I think we can be involved in and leverage others to be involved, I try to do it."

THE PEP RALLY

You don't have to possess a lot of money to give to others. All you need is a big heart and a desire to help. It's easy to sit back and let high-profile coaches and players do the work. For them, it can be easier because they have a larger platform, and the publicity looks good, although that is not necessarily the motivation.

But it doesn't take much to make a positive difference in someone's life.

Do you pass people on the streets who are in need? Have your heartstrings been tugged by a commercial for a children's hospital? Do you want to help financially or as a volunteer, or are you satisfied to let others make an impact?

THE BIG DANCE

I don't have the resources of Tim Tebow, but each year I put on my tuxedo and shine shoes for attendees of the Tim Tebow Night to Shine Prom for people with special needs. It doesn't cost me a dime to give three hours of my time. And when it's over, the feeling of making someone smile is priceless.

Do some research, find a cause near and dear to your heart, and get involved.

You pay nothing to serve the homeless at a soup kitchen, but the time spent is priceless. A good friend of mine has done this every Wednesday for several years. She never misses it, and she is rewarded with internal satisfaction. In other words, it makes her feel good.

Think about taking a snack to nurses at a hospice unit some evening or becoming a Big Brother or Big Sister volunteer—and stick with your commitment.

If you are blessed with financial resources, consider making a donation to a charity that does fantastic work, like Samaritan's Purse, Samaritan's Feet, or the Salvation Army.

There are many organizations that need help. If you can't find one you like, start your own foundation to help high school students earn a scholarship or support another cause that is meaningful to you.

Take a mission trip to a developing country to help build a well, a school, or a church. If you are a physician, consider providing free medical assistance at clinics in impoverished neighborhoods. If you're healthy, consider donating blood.

There are countless things you can do, but you must have the desire to help.

If you have the funds, consider becoming a donor. And if you don't, give something more valuable—your time.

Make the Big Blue Nation proud.

Are you charitable? How can you make a difference?

_____

_____

_____

_____

WEEK 12 | REDEMPTION

KENTUCKY FANS LOOKING FOR A feel-good redemption story will certainly remember the plight of Scott Padgett. The 6'9" standout from St. Xavier High School in Louisville was recruited by Rick Pitino to play college basketball for the University of Kentucky.

During much of his freshman season in 1994, Padgett was chained to the bench, averaging a pedestrian 2 points and 1.2 rebounds while logging only fifty-seven minutes through fourteen games. Off the court, his first year was beset with academic problems. Rumors abounded that Padgett, who was openly flaunting his status as a UK Basketball player as a means to get by in the classroom, was just one misstep away from flunking out completely.

Padgett sat out the entire 1995–1996 championship season due to his continuing academic woes, but he returned the following year with a new work ethic and improved attitude. By the time his junior season rolled around, Padgett was firmly entrenched in the starting lineup on a team in the hunt for another championship title.

Ever since Christian Laettner nailed the dagger into the heart of BBN in the 1992 NCAA tournament, Kentucky fans had been actively seeking revenge against the hated Blue Devils. Their chance finally came six years later in the NCAA South regionals in St. Petersburg, Florida.

Padgett, together with returning veterans Jeff Sheppard, Nazr Mohammed, and Wayne Turner, comprised a number-two-seeded UK squad that seemed eager to take on the top-seeded team from Durham.

Duke, sporting future first-round NBA draft picks Elton Brand, Shane Battier, and William Avery, would be no pushover. In the first half, the Blue Devils scalded the nets with a 17–0 run, shooting over 54 percent from the field as they jumped out to a comfortable 49–39 lead.

The second half saw Duke slowly extend its cushion. After a basket off an offensive rebound, Mike Krzyzewski's squad suddenly found itself up 71–54 with just 9:38 to go. It appeared that revenge and redemption for this group of Wildcats was not to be.

Not so fast, my friend. A trifecta of three-pointers—one each by Heshimu Evans, Padgett, and Allen Edwards—cut the deficit down in the blink of an eye. During that same run, Turner schooled Duke guard Steve Wojciechowski on several consecutive drives to the bucket—and before you knew it, the Cats were only down 72–71 with six minutes still to play.

Cameron Mills's three-point bomb—his first basket of the tournament—gave Kentucky its first lead at 80–79 with 2:15 to play. With Duke out of time-outs, the Cats went for broke.

With the score tied at 81 and under a minute to go, Turner curled off a high pick from Padgett. As Duke rushed to cut off Turner, they left Padgett open at the top of the key. Turner swung the ball back to Padgett, whose high-arching three with 39.4 seconds remaining hit nothing but net. That "three-pointer heard around the world" gave Kentucky just enough of a cushion for an 86–84 win. The Laettner demons had finally been exorcized.

A little more than a week later, Kentucky would go on to beat Utah 78–69 in San Antonio for their eighth national title. As unexpected as that championship was for most Wildcat fans, what Padgett accomplished in the classroom was even more remarkable. The guy who nearly flunked out became a two-time academic All-SEC selection.

The story doesn't end there, though. Scott Padgett was selected as the twenty-eighth overall pick in the first round of the 1999 NBA draft. He went on to play ten seasons with four different NBA teams. After his playing career ended, he served six seasons as head coach of the Samford Bulldogs.

Who would have believed it? It just goes to show you what hard work and a changed mindset can do.

THE COMEBACK

Have you been in a situation where you have great potential, but you have failed to meet the expectations of your family, friends, colleagues, and even yourself?

At one time, you had dreams of making it big, landing that perfect job with the corner office, driving a cool car, and having a gorgeous spouse.

But somewhere along the way, you did not stick with the game plan. You thought you could rely on the reputation of your parents or the heavy influence of a friend to get you where you wanted to be in life.

Reality has sunk in, and you haven't gotten to play as much as you thought you should. You have been on the bench for several years. Your sense of entitlement did not prepare you to put in the hard work it takes to be successful. But there is still time.

THE OVERTIME WIN

You might be in a tough circumstance, and your support system might not expect a championship banner, but you can surprise them and bring home a big win.

Go back and finish your education. Apply for the job you feel underqualified for, and then do your homework to prepare for a great interview. Make an attempt to talk to the loved one you have not spoken to for the past few years, apologize, and make things right.

This is on you. The time to complain is over. It's gameday. The only two things you can control are your attitude and your effort.

Will you get the job? Can you get your life back on track? Is there a way to correct the wrongs? Yes. Will it be easy? No.

But don't let the demons of the past prevent you from making a run to cut down the nets.

Scott Padgett saw the writing on the wall and was determined not to let the opportunity of a lifetime slam dunk over him. You can do the same. Redemption is a comeback story. It's the action of saving or being saved from sin, error, or evil.

Your story is far from over. You can put together a run and hit the game-winning shots.

The next best thing to beating Duke is pulling off the upset win in life!

Go Big Blue.

How can you make a comeback?

WEEK 13 | WE'RE NOT IN KANSAS ANYMORE

IT'S THE SYSTEM, STUPID! MANY would blame the "system" for what happened on the night of December 9, 1989, in Allen Fieldhouse in Lawrence, Kansas. Probation-riddled Kentucky, under first-year head coach Rick Pitino, was in way over its head on its path to a record-setting 150–95 blowout loss to the Jayhawks. Granted, Kansas—under Coach Roy Williams—had a fabulous team that year, but it was Pitino's insistence on sticking to his system that resulted in the humiliation of a 55-point defeat.

Pitino's system involved pressing the opposition into submission. Even if you didn't make the steal, relentless full-court pressure can wear your opponent down. Unfortunately for Pitino, Kansas, buoyed by the energy of a rabid home crowd, broke the press at will early on in jumping out to an inconceivable 80–61 halftime lead. A stubborn Pitino elected to continue pressing Kansas throughout the remainder of the game, even after the outcome had long been decided. It was a calculated ploy intended to signal his team right from the outset that this was the style they were going to play. *Better get in shape, boys—come hell or high water, we got some pressin' to do!*

Kentucky, which started the game with only eight scholarship players, ended the game with three players having fouled out and three more saddled with four fouls apiece. Obviously shorthanded, Pitino insisted on turning up the heat. Even Roy Williams tried to convince him to back off in the latter stages of the game, but Rick would have none of it. The system was the system, and he believed in it despite the public beatdown.

Pitino, who picked up two technical fouls during the contest, was noticeably upset afterward. He proceeded to kick everyone out of the locker room—including Bill Keightley, UK's long-time equipment manager—as he visibly vented his frustration by knocking over water bottles.

"After that game, it was vintage Coach Pitino," said Sean Woods, the starting point guard and one of the future "Unforgettables." "I think he was more disappointed because, in his eyes, it felt like we just gave in—getting beat by 55."

Almost exactly a year later, on December 8, 1990, in Rupp Arena, Kentucky would exact revenge. Although falling significantly short of the point differential of the previous contest, the Wildcats still dominated the Jayhawks to the tune of an 88–71 shellacking. Woods had a career night, with 25 points on 11 of 15 shooting—to go along with 8 assists, 6 rebounds, and 3 steals. As a team, Kentucky's full-court pressure forced 21 Jayhawk turnovers and resulted in 10 total steals.

"[That] was the revenge deal against Kansas," Sean admitted. "We didn't forget about that killing we got the year before. Coach really put emphasis on how to stop them. We wanted to at least beat them by 25. I don't think we did, but we wanted to beat them—and we did."

Of course, this game was only the beginning of the legend of the "Unforgettables"—the team that would later go on to capture the hearts of the fan base with their exciting style of running, three-point shooting, and relentless full-court pressure. Pitino's system had survived, thrived, and would prove itself over time.

And to think it all began with a total system failure on a cold December night in the rolling plains of Kansas.

THE MARATHON WORKOUT

Everyone faces failures in life, but how do you respond? Do you give up and quit, or do you try even harder the next time to meet the challenge head-on?

What obstacles are in your way?

Maybe you are striving to make good grades in school, and you feel the pressure mounting because you are not performing well in the classroom.

Perhaps your job is on the line, layoffs are predicted, and you have a family to feed and bills to pay.

Or did your doctor blindside you with an unexpected diagnosis either for you or someone close to you?

Is life beating you down and getting worse no matter how hard you work to try to fix it?

You are not alone.

Perhaps you feel like giving up, and you feel that putting the pressure on the entire game was a total waste of time. When you get home, do you feel like throwing a Coach Pitino fit?

THE SWEET TASTE OF VICTORY

No matter how difficult your struggles are with everyday life, you must stay positive.

Virginia Satir said it best: "Life is not the way it's supposed to be, it's the way it is. The way you cope is what makes the difference."

When life gets rough, and the opponent is scoring at will, you have a choice to make: you can either take the negative approach by making excuses and quitting or you can be positive and keep fighting.

Does that mean all your problems will go away? No. But it helps you to handle them better and find a way to cope. Make a point to set your attitude early in the day with some inspirational quotes or a devotional handbook. A positive attitude is the first step to overcoming negative circumstances.

Another way to fight your way through your struggles is to accept what has happened and move on. There will be times when you cannot change your circumstances, and you will have to face the outcome—much like the Wildcats did when Kansas beat them down. But UK used this experience as motivation to come back the next year and prevail.

Redeem your past failures by using your defeat as an inspiration to achieve future success.

Learn from your past mistakes and be grateful for another chance. All things happen for a reason, and perhaps your past defeat is a blessing in disguise that in the end will give you a better life. If you have the right mindset, you can affect the outcome for the good. Just keep working hard.

Go Cats.

How can you overcome a big loss?

_____

_____

_____

_____

_____

_____

_____

EARLY SEASON
LAUNCH

WEEK 14 | THE PRINCE WHO WOULD BE KING

IMAGINE HITTING A THREE-POINTER IN front of 23,153 screaming fans in Rupp Arena. Now imagine hitting four more of them in a row on five consecutive possessions within a two-minute span to begin the game. Improbable as that sounds, that's exactly what happened to Tayshaun Prince on Saturday, December 8, 2001.

Tayshaun's fifth three-pointer was launched from nearly twenty-eight feet, right at the edge of the UK midcourt logo. It staked the Wildcats to an early lead, which eventually propelled eleventh-ranked Kentucky to a comfortable 79–59 win over the North Carolina Tar Heels. As you might expect, Prince's fifth consecutive three-pointer nearly blew the roof off of Rupp Arena. Talk about being *in the zone*. Many in the house claimed it's the loudest Rupp has ever been.

Tayshaun ended up with a career-high 31 points on 11 of 22 shooting (7 of 11 on three-pointers) that evening. Amazingly, he hit his first 7 shots, 6 of them from behind the arc. He also pulled down 11 rebounds, dished out 4 assists, and had 4 steals as part of Kentucky's 1,800th win in school history.

"It was a remarkable feeling," said the lanky 6'9" string bean of a player from Compton, California. "To hit 4 or 5 shots to get the team going in a game like this, against North Carolina, that's something as a little kid you dream about."

"I've never seen anything like that in all my days of basketball," said his coach, Tubby Smith. "He was just possessed. His radar and where he was shooting them from were just unbelievable."

Tayshaun's quiet, laidback demeanor belied the grand accomplishments of his UK career. From the 1999 through the 2002 season, Prince scored 1,775 total points, which places him eighth on the all-time UK scoring list, between Kevin Grevey and Cotton Nash. His 204 three-pointers are the third-most in school history. In addition, he captured All-American honors twice, was a three-time All-SEC selection, and was the SEC Player of the Year in 2001.

After his junior season, Prince declared for the NBA draft but withdrew his name in order to return for his senior season. Although he averaged 17.5 points per contest, led the team in rebounding with just over 6 per game, and scored 41 in the NCAA tournament game against Tulsa, that was the year of "Team Turmoil"—the Tubby Smith–coached group of misfits that couldn't get along and miserably underachieved.

Drafted number twenty-three overall in the first round of the 2002 NBA draft by the Detroit Pistons, Tayshaun went on to have a solid seventeen-year professional career. Throw in an Olympic gold medal in 2008, and you can see why he's a favorite among fans who remember his three-point barrage versus the Tar Heels.

CBS announcer Bill Raftery said it best on the television broadcast that day: "Tayshaun is not a prince, he's a king!"

PRACTICE MAKES PERFECT

It's a cliché, but it has been proven over time to be true: you play how you practice.

If you go into your workout with a lethargic effort, more than likely that's how you will perform under pressure.

I am not sure if Tayshaun practiced hitting five three-pointers in a row, but he certainly had been working on his shot his entire life.

There is validity when players enter the "zone." I remember when Larry Bird won the first three-point shooting contest in 1985 at the NBA All-Star game. Early in the final round, the Hick from French Lick hit 11 consecutive trifectas and scored 23 out of 30.

The zone. He was there. It had to be a good feeling.

Tayshaun had the same feeling. The basket must have looked as big as a hula hoop.

You may not be in Rupp Arena and have the opportunity to give your team a shot in the arm like Tayshaun did, but there are ways you can get off to a hot start in everyday life.

IN THE ZONE

No one is always at their best.

Some days are smooth sailing, but on the not so good days, when you might face discouragement and unexpected challenges, you need to be at your best.

Get off to a good start. Be thankful for life by demonstrating an attitude of gratitude. Begin with an inspirational read or a devotion to get your mind ready for the day's challenges. Listen to an upbeat podcast or even think about starting your own.

Be centered and focused on what is important. Greet your spouse and children with a smile and hug.

Your perspective sets the tone for everyone in your home and workplace. Make sure people don't dread hearing you come down the stairs or into the office.

Make sure your priorities are in check. If you need to return some calls or emails when you get to work, do it as soon as you arrive. Never put off what can be done now, because the last thing you want to do is get behind.

Tayshaun put North Carolina into a hole, and those Tar Heels never climbed out. You can win too by getting off to a fast start.

Meet your fears head-on and relax when uncomfortable circumstances arise. It's okay if your day does not go as planned and obstacles seem to come out of nowhere. Be flexible and rise to the challenge. Keep your cool and focus on what's important.

Don't let unpleasant situations put you on the bench. Avoid overreacting and try to make something positive happen. Call a time-out and huddle up to develop a game plan.

Get plenty of rest, and plan for each day to be the best one ever. Then go out and hit the five shots to get everyone around you in a good mood.

How can you get into the zone?

_____

_____

_____

_____

_____

_____

_____

_____

_____

_____

_____

_____

_____

_____

WEEK 15 | NOTHING BUT A "BLUR"

WHEN YOU'RE DOWN 6 POINTS with only thirty-one seconds to go in overtime, it's usually a signal for the home fans to head for the exits. On Saturday, December 9, 1978, the Wildcats found themselves in just that position, down 66–60 to the fifth-ranked Kansas Jayhawks in Rupp Arena. Kentucky guards Truman Claytor and Jay Shidler had already fouled out, leaving Big Blue fans little reason to think a victory was remotely possible. Remember, this was the era before the three-point shot. Kentucky would need a miracle to avoid its first loss of the young season.

That miracle came in the form of Dwight Anderson, a 6'3" superstar hoops talent from Dayton, Ohio. Up to that point in the game, the freshman guard—the number-one-ranked recruit in the country that year—had played only ten minutes and hadn't scored a single point. With Kentucky's backs against the wall, however, Anderson finally delivered by driving the lane, scoring, and cutting the Kansas lead to 66–62.

Defensively, with desperation setting in, the Cats scrambled frantically to deny the inbounds pass. With just sixteen ticks remaining on the game clock, and fearful of a five-second violation, Kansas's Darnell Valentine allegedly pushed Anderson in the back in an attempt to get open. Valentine was immediately whistled for an offensive foul.

Anderson went to the foul line and missed the front end of the one-and-one. Kentucky grabbed the rebound and missed the put back, but Anderson somehow corralled the loose ball and was fouled in the act of shooting with only ten seconds left on the clock.

This time, Anderson drilled both free throws, cutting the Kansas lead to 66–64. Still, all Kansas had to do was inbounds the ball successfully and that would be all she wrote.

But again, it was Anderson to the rescue. He knocked loose the ensuing Kansas inbounds pass. The ball bounced over to Kyle Macy on the left wing, who drilled the fifteen-foot jumper to knot the score with four seconds left. In the chaos that ensued, Kansas called for a time-out that they did not have. That resulted in a technical foul and free throw. The always-dependable Macy stepped up to the line and calmly sank the charity toss to complete the improbable 7–0 run to steal the victory.

Dwight "The Blur" Anderson was one of the fastest players to ever wear the Kentucky uniform. There may have been quicker players, but there was no one who could go from one end of the court to the other faster than him. Dwight was "John Wall fast" long before there was even a John Wall. In that initial 1978–1979 season, Anderson was UK's second leading scorer, averaging 13.3 points per game. His breakout performance occurred in the seventh game of the season against number-two-ranked Notre Dame, when he torched the Irish with 17 points in just nineteen minutes of action in Kentucky's 81–76 upset victory in Freedom Hall. That prompted ex-Marquette coach Al McGuire, serving as a color analyst for the NBC broadcast, to famously proclaim that "a star is born."

Then, before Kentucky fans could bat an eye, "Dwight Lightning" was gone, having transferred to Southern Cal in December of his sophomore season amid much rumor and speculation.

After a decent college career at USC—where he averaged 20 points and was All-Pac-10 First Team—Anderson was selected by the then–Washington Bullets in the second round of the 1982 NBA draft. After five failed tryouts with other NBA teams, he bounced around the Continental Basketball Association, spent two seasons overseas in the Philippines, and then had a very short stint with the hometown Dayton Wings of the World Basketball League.

Drug abuse problems led to a period of homelessness before rehabilitation in 2004 at the Houston-based John Lucas Treatment Center got Anderson's personal life back on track.

Tragically, Anderson died suddenly on September 5, 2020. Looking back on his life, it's sad to see how a career that seemed destined for NBA stardom was ultimately derailed by what Anderson later acknowledged as his battle with drug and alcohol addiction.

Dwight Anderson was only fifty-nine years old when he died. Just like the last thirty-one seconds of the comeback versus Kansas, his time on earth seemed like nothing but a blur.

NO TIME-OUTS LEFT

Do you ever look around and wonder, "Where has all the time gone?"

Have you spent so much time at work that you have missed out on how fast your kids have grown? What were your priorities?

Or somewhere along the way did you become dependent on either prescription or illegal drugs and lose your way? In your ambition to climb the ladder to the top, did you lose your focus by spending more time socializing at the local bar instead of going home to your family?

Maybe the bottle became your friend during times of loneliness, and friends are nowhere to be found when times get tough.

Or perhaps your addiction is something else. Whatever steals your time and resources and puts the health of your relationships at risk falls into this category.

Before you know what has happened, *poof!* You have lost everything.

Now what?

THE PUT BACK SHOT

Don't wait until you hit rock-bottom before you make a change.

The first step in fighting an addiction is the toughest, and that is to admit you have a problem.

Be adult enough to put your ego aside and your loved ones first.

Consider making a change and seeking professional and spiritual help.

No one will, or should, condemn you, especially if you want to improve yourself.

Don't let your potential go unfulfilled. Your life might be just tipping off, and you have the rest of the game to play. Or it may be in the final few minutes, and you trail your opponent.

In either case, you have time to pull out the win. But you must want it bad enough to make the change.

Don't let your life be a blur that's over too soon.

Go Big Blue.

What changes can you make if you have an addiction?

Do you want help?

WEEK 16 | THE LAST CALL

NO BOOK ON KENTUCKY BASKETBALL would be complete without a chapter on Cawood Ledford. From 1953 through 1992, the Harlan native served as the play-by-play "Voice of the Wildcats." For thirty-nine years, his iconic radio presence graced our homes and blessed our lives with those highly descriptive calls Kentucky fans have come to treasure and love.

"Hello, everybody. This is Cawood Ledford," he'd begin. Then for the next couple of hours, the legendary Hall of Fame broadcaster would hold court with his impassioned audience—their emotions, reactions, and excitement hanging fervidly on his every word. Some of the fondest childhood memories between father and son were made sitting together by the radio listening to Cawood and Ralph (Hacker) call those epic games.

To many, Cawood was larger than life. To see him out in public with cigarette in hand made you goggle-eyed and speechless. For Kentucky fans, he was bigger than Elvis. Man, that rich, resonant voice—I bet you can hear it right now: "Kentucky moving from right to left on your radio dial."

One of the reasons Cawood was so special was because he felt like one of us. You knew he wanted Kentucky to win, but he wasn't afraid to tell it like it was, either. If the Cats weren't playing well, Cawood would call them out. You trusted Cawood to paint the picture of what happened on the court. Whatever did transpire—whether ecstasy or agony—we all knew Cawood would be there to keep us grounded.

What many Kentucky fans forget is that Cawood's broadcasting reach and talent extended well beyond the court at Rupp Arena named in his honor. Many experts actually believed that horse racing was his best sport. For many years, he did the CBS Radio call for the Kentucky Derby. In addition, baseball's World Series, golf's The Masters, boxing matches involving Muhammad Ali, and, of course, the NCAA tournament all made his heralded list of personal achievements. Always splendidly dressed, Cawood was a professional's professional.

Appropriately, Cawood's last call came on March 28, 1992—the infamous 104–103 overtime loss to Duke in the NCAA East regional finals at the Spectrum in Philadelphia. It was a crushing defeat for Kentucky fans but a heck of a way for Cawood to go out in a blaze of glory. Even Duke coach Mike Krzyzewski took time out in the midst of his team's postgame celebration to approach Cawood and congratulate him on a fabulous career.

When it came time to retire, Cawood wanted to make sure he went out at the top of his game. How do you sign off after nearly forty transcendent years in the business? The former World War II marine, Centre College graduate, and Hall High School English teacher from Booger Hollow did it the only way he knew how—with class, dignity, and humility.

"For those of you who have gone down the glory road with me, my eternal thanks. This is Cawood Ledford saying goodbye, God bless, and goodnight, everybody."

PREGAME NOTES

Everyone wants to leave a positive legacy. Cawood did that like none other in his business. He did it with dedication, integrity, and sacrifice. Sacrifice? What did he sacrifice? He traveled with the Cats. How can that be a sacrifice?

For one, he spent many nights away from home. And to be at the top of his game, he had to spend hours preparing and planning before and after games. The life of a sportscaster can be a blast, but it can also be lonely on the road.

While you may never call an overtime loss in the NCAA regional finals to end your career, your life can make an impact on others, and your family and friends will remember and honor you.

Making a difference takes commitment and giving up some things you value as precious. It takes a sacrifice.

What can you do to make a difference?

TURN ON THE MICROPHONE

Your first priority should be a desire to do good. Help others because you love them, not to obtain any glory.

Volunteer your time. This is a great way to give back to your community. Most of the time this is not glamorous—you might serve food at a soup kitchen or become active in a local civic organization. The sacrifice here could mean taking a weekend to help people instead of taking the boat out on the lake.

Give blood. This can actually save the life of someone who needs to have heart surgery or is battling leukemia. And the best part is that the recipient will never know who helped them. That can be a humbling feeling.

Become a mentor at a Big Brother or Big Sister organization or at an after-school facility. Even if you only volunteer two or three days a month, the impact you can have on a life is immeasurable. The sacrifice of your time is a valuable investment.

Participate in or organize an event for a local charity. This could be a simple auction, golf tournament, or even a high-profile dinner program with a celebrity speaker. The point here is to become involved in something bigger than yourself. Ask your family and friends to pitch in—they can have a blast while doing a good deed.

Support local activities. Volunteer to clean up after high school football games or take the lead role in a local play. Become active in community meetings and clubs or aspire to be a local leader in your community. You don't have to possess wealth and resources to be valuable. Just be involved.

You can take part in countless activities to leave a positive and lasting legacy, but it takes dedication. When you become active, stay involved. Make the commitment. Make it a point to become the unofficial face of a cause that you adopt.

Your sacrifices will benefit others and give them hope. Be sure to keep your priorities in order.

And if you think it's too late, you're wrong. Get started.

Big Blue Nation.

How will people remember you?

What can you do to make an impact?

WEEK 17 | DREAM GAME
TURNED NIGHTMARE

THE MOST ANTICIPATED KENTUCKY BASKETBALL game in the history of the state took place in—of all places—Tennessee. On March 26, 1983, number-twelve-ranked Kentucky battled number-two-ranked Louisville in Knoxville. The 12,489 lucky fans that crowded into the Stokely Athletics Center on the UT campus witnessed a rarity that day. Prior to that date, the Cats and Cards hadn't met on the court in over twenty-four years as a result of some prideful and petty gamesmanship from parties on both sides.

Louisville coach Denny Crum had lobbied hard for an annual regular-season matchup between the two schools. He had already won a national title in 1980 and was looking to further boost credibility within the state. Kentucky coach Joe B. Hall, on the other hand, wanted to avoid playing Louisville at all cost. He felt like he had nothing to gain. Playing Louisville wasn't what Adolph Rupp had intended, and Joe was adamant about upholding the tradition.

As fate would have it, the two teams were placed on a collision course in the same bracket of the NCAA Mideast regional. Because it was so unlikely, pundits proclaimed it the "dream game." Fans holding tickets to the contest felt like they had won the lottery. The Cats versus Cards was going to be a sight to behold.

The dream began with Kentucky jumping out to an early 23–10 lead behind the hot shooting of Derrick Hord and Jim Master. Louisville slowly chipped away and closed to within 37–30 at the half. At the 16:38 mark of the second half, Kentucky was still up 43–32 when the Cardinals turned up the full-court pressure. Within a five-minute span, Louisville not only erased the entire deficit but took a 50–49 lead on a Lancaster Gordon–led fast-break bucket.

With seventeen seconds to play and the score tied at 60, Dirk Minniefield went back door for what looked like a game-winning play. But Charles Jones of Louisville tipped the ball away at the last moment. Gordon grabbed it and drove for a layup, giving Louisville a 62–60 lead with just ten seconds to play.

After a Kentucky time-out, the Wildcats tried to set up a shot for Melvin Turpin near the basket. With all eyes on Turpin, Jim Master was able to sneak down the sideline for the game-tying twelve-footer. Pandemonium erupted within the entire Kentucky contingent. They had grabbed the momentum heading into overtime and had what they thought would be the victory in hand.

But it wasn't to be. Gordon went nuts in the overtime, and Louisville outscored Kentucky 18–6 for an emotionally draining 80–68 victory. For Kentucky fans in attendance, the dream game had suddenly turned into a nightmare. The dreaded drive back to Lexington in the middle of the night would seem like the longest three hours of their lives.

Fortunately for Kentucky and Louisville Basketball fans, the dream game was not one and done; it has now become an annual regular-season event. Due to the intensity and passion of both their fan bases, it has morphed into arguably the number-one rivalry in all of college basketball.

MAKE OUT THE SCHEDULE

Every day you are faced with a choice: you can stay in bed and dream dreams, or you can get up, get ready, and chase them.

What you aspire to be is unique—just like you. You might consider following in the footsteps of a mentor, or you could have your own ambitions. Either way, it is up to you.

Some people do not try to chase their dreams because they are afraid of failure. They relegate their lives to a routine instead of living an adventure. They let their fear of the unknown discourage them from moving forward.

At times, there may be moments and circumstances you can't control that dictate your future. Maybe you had to find a job at a young age to help support your family. Or perhaps you had to step into a parental role due to a parent's illness or addiction.

Nevertheless, don't give up on your dreams. They provide the hope you need to reach your goals.

THE ANNUAL GAME

Perhaps your situation is not ideal but be inspired to dig deeper for the motivation to succeed.

Don't be afraid to explore and research to develop your goals. If you're embarrassed by your lack of knowledge, take the initiative to explore and arm yourself with the facts.

Ask questions of people who have traveled a similar journey and look to them for mentorship.

Have courage and believe in yourself as you push for success. If you don't fight for yourself, you will live with regrets.

Kentucky fans love the Louisville rivalry because someone had the audacity to put it on the schedule.

Take a risk or a long shot. Famed hockey legend Wayne Gretzky said, "You miss 100 percent of the shots you don't take."

This doesn't mean to just fire away randomly at whatever you can hit. Make a calculated attempt to hit your goal. Failure is the result of a lack of commitment to act.

Instead of just daydreaming, plan a concrete strategy. When you make plans, you actually have a purpose and something to execute. A daydream is just wishful thinking.

Maintain a positive attitude and go after your dreams. It's okay if they are big. Norman Vincent Peale said, "Shoot for the moon. Even if you miss, you'll land among the stars."

Never accept failure. There will be roadblocks and obstacles along the way. These challenges will only make your dream sweeter when it becomes reality.

And if for some reason you don't hit your mark, it's okay. Putting forth the effort is what is most important.

Believe in yourself and strive to be a better person each day. Never, ever give up. When you combine a plan with confidence in your ability to reach your destination, you set yourself up for a big chase. Enjoy the ride.

Go Big Blue.

How can you put yourself in a situation to make your dreams come true?

_____

_____

_____

_____

_____

_____

_____

_____

WEEK 18 | YOU CAN'T GO HOME AGAIN

THE SECOND-MOST ANTICIPATED KENTUCKY BASKET-BALL game in the history of the state took place on Saturday, December 29, 2001. Rick Pitino was returning to Camelot, and Kentucky fans were hyped beyond imagination. After his failed stint in the NBA, Pitino was back in the college ranks. Of all the places he could have landed, he chose the University of Louisville—UK's most hated archrival.

The game didn't quite live up to the atmosphere surrounding it as the sixth-ranked Wildcats rolled over their unranked neighbors by a lopsided score of 82–62. Kentucky shook off a cold shooting start to grab a modest 36–32 lead at the half. Second-half spurts of 16–2 and 15–0 would eventually put the game away. Tayshaun Prince and Keith Bogans led Kentucky in scoring with 18 and 17 points, respectively.

But it was Traitor Rick's return that generated all the buzz.

When Rick Pitino became Louisville's head coach a year earlier, the floodgates opened to a torrent of pent-up emotions from the UK fan base. Admiration for the man who saved the program when he took over in 1989 was suddenly replaced with outright contempt. For fans who valued loyalty, what Rick did was unforgivable.

They appreciated what he accomplished at UK, but they never understood anyone turning Benedict Arnold. You don't sleep with the enemy, stab your former employer in the back, or marry your ex-wife's best friend. Once a Wildcat, always a Wildcat.

That was the problem. Rick was never really a Wildcat. Even when Little Ricky was leading Kentucky to the 1996 national championship, many Kentucky fans regarded him as just a displaced big-city dude thinking he was doing the local hayseeds a giant favor. This dismissive mindset and his massive ego would eventually land him in deep trouble at U of L, with his well-documented indiscretions—marital infidelity, strippers in the dorm, and the ongoing FBI probe—resulting in a rapid demise.

Retired army general Colin Powell once said, "Power corrupts, but absolute power is . . . pretty darn neat." That's what happened to Pitino and the rest of the Louisville heads of state. They became intoxicated with power and operated as if they were above the law. They succumbed to the soothing serenade of their sycophants and honestly believed that they were pooping ice cream.

Kentucky fans certainly don't condone any of what Pitino was accused of doing. Lying, cheating, infidelity, greed, and pride are never the keys to success. The University of Louisville was completely correct in letting him go. Many were surprised they didn't fire him sooner.

If they're completely honest, though, Kentucky fans miss Rick Pitino. They miss his demonic scowl, the spittle flying from his lips, and his deathly pale countenance as he pranced along the Rupp Arena sidelines. They miss his custom Armani suits, brazenly red tie, and perfectly dyed hair, and they miss watching him yell animatedly at his minions while condescendingly berating the men in striped shirts.

There's something gratifying about watching Pitino's obligatory postgame handshake with John Calipari after another devastating loss—envy, resentment, and bitterness oozing from every one of his jealous pores after losing eight out of their ten games played. In fact, BBN misses all the vitriol, venom, and vindictiveness suddenly absent from one of the best rivalries in college basketball. Because without Rick as the villain, you simply can't hate Louisville anymore.

IN THE FILM ROOM

Loyalty is a simple word that packs a powerful meaning. It means to have a "strong feeling of support or allegiance." Trust can take many years to develop but only one minute to destroy—similar to a reputation. The two go hand in hand.

Even the very word can stir up emotions.

From motion pictures to novels to personal relationships, the most endearing quality is loyalty.

That's why people love dogs and children. Their allegiance goes without question.

But betrayal is destructive and leaves scars for years to come.

True loyalty is decorated in respect. It's knowing that someone has your back.

Have you ever broken the trust of someone? Chances are you have.

Do you remember the pain you caused? Was the person you betrayed hurt? Is there any way to heal?

HOMECOMING

In sports, wins breed loyalty. If a player or coach can produce victories, then all is often forgotten.

But that is not the case with personal betrayal. Can you restore faith after you have hurt someone? Yes, you can. Will it be easy? No, but if you really love someone, it is worth it to put in the hard work.

Be patient. Once trust is compromised, it can take a while to build it back. But it can happen. Don't be in a hurry and expect someone to recover from the pain in a few days.

You must show remorse when you hurt someone. Be sensitive to their feelings and be willing to invest the time and effort needed to prove yourself again.

If you are the person who gets hurt, you must decide for yourself if extending forgiveness is worth the risk.

If a loved one keeps hurting you over and over, you may want to evaluate the situation. Professional help might be in order.

Honor your commitments, and make sure that you make everyone close to you feel special.

Can you go home again? Yes.

Would BBN welcome back Rick Pitino if there was a coaching vacancy? Doubt it, but perhaps—you never know.

Go home.

Go Big Blue.

How can you make strides to show more loyalty to your family and friends?

_____
_____
_____
_____
_____
_____
_____
_____
_____
_____
_____
_____

WEEK 19 | THE LITTLE BROTHER WHO COULDN'T

"LOUISVILLE IS LIKE THE LITTLE brother fighting for recognition from the big brother."

Ever since Eddie Sutton uttered those immortal words back in December 1986, the Kentucky-Louisville rivalry has been rocketing toward basketball Armageddon. Understandably, Eddie's quip rankled many in the Cardinals' camp—and for the next three and a half decades, Louisville fans have simmered like a petulant younger sibling, trying desperately to bury that well-fitting moniker.

On the basketball court, it seemed that anything the Cards did, the Cats would do better. Big brother routinely pounded little brother into submission while rubbing Junior's nose in the humiliating stench of multiple defeats.

From Cedric Jenkins's last-second tip (1987–1988), to Patrick Sparks's game-winning shuffle (2004–2005), to DeMarcus Cousins going WWE on Jared Shropshire's face (2009–2010), to Anthony Davis's Final Four dominance (2011–2012), to Tyler Ulis's bloody-eyed stare (2014–2015), to John Calipari's mastery over Rick Pitino, it seemed like Kentucky fans always had plenty to celebrate.

But if there's an iconic big brother moment in the history of the rivalry, King Rex dropping 26 points in the 85–51 rout of little brother on December 27, 1986, has to be at the top of everybody's list.

Rex Chapman, the 6'4" boy wonder from Owensboro, was one of a kind. Heavily recruited out of Apollo High School, he could do it all—run, shoot, pass, jump, and dunk. He could school you down low or step back and bury the three. Put simply, Rex had game. Surprisingly, he grew up cheering for Louisville, so Kentucky fans breathed a sigh of relief when he finally signed with the Cats.

As a freshman, Rex torched the Cardinals for 26 points during their annual holiday showdown. For the game, he shot 10 for 20 from the field (on 5 of 8 three-pointers), had 4 assists, 2 steals, and added a memorable monster dunk in front of a demoralized Freedom Hall crowd. Those watching back in "Rexington" knew it was the start of something special.

Unfortunately for Kentucky fans statewide, his time wearing blue ended way too quickly. After the last game of his sophomore season—an 80–74 loss to Villanova in the third round of the 1987 NCAA tournament—everyone knew that Rex was gone. He declared early for the NBA draft and was selected with the eighth pick in the first round by the Charlotte Hornets. He ended up having a decent—but not great—twelve-year NBA career, averaging just under 15 points per game.

A lot happened to Rex after his playing days were over. He faced some arduous challenges and battled some difficult demons. He worked hard on his path to recovery—speaking openly about his addiction to opioids. In the process, he became a social media sensation.

But even with all he's been through, one thing stands out for Kentucky fans. They'll always remember Rex for the time he put that king-sized whoopin' on his pesky little brother.

BUILD THE ROSTER

If you have more than one child, or brothers and sisters, chances are you've experienced some tense moments of drama. Even the closest siblings can get on each other's nerves and cause friction.

Do your children accuse you of playing favorites or treating others better than them? Or maybe you even pointed the finger at your own parents for the same reasons.

In the television show *Everybody Loves Raymond*, the older brother, Robert, is convinced that his parents love his younger brother, Raymond, more than him.

In the sitcom, Raymond gets everything while Robert gets dumped on by his parents.

Can you relate? Does this scenario hit home with you?

Perhaps you never intended to give more attention to one child than another, but your kids don't see it that way. Or maybe you felt that way while growing up.

Sibling rivalry does happen. Fights can break out over anything: deciding what to watch on TV, choosing a restaurant, following the rules, and much more.

I grew up the youngest of four boys. All my brothers, to this day, tell me I was Mom's favorite. I think they're right, and that is okay with me.

Does it bother you that your kids might have this impression? How did they come to this conclusion?

Or do your brothers and sisters feel this way about you?

MAKE THE CUTS

As a parent, it's important that you do your best to foster a good relationship between your children. Treat your kids with the same unconditional love, and work to resolve any conflicts that can damage their relationships with each other.

Promote and encourage ways for them to listen to each other calmly without yelling. Show them how to engage in conversation where everyone gets their say.

Learn how to handle disputes in a way that is fair and keeps your authority in proper perspective.

Explain to your kids that the family is like a team. They all have roles to play, and each must attend practice and work hard. No one gets more glory or recognition than the other, and you all work together for the same prizes—peace and joy.

Step in when needed but try to let your children fight their own battles. Don't take a side in front of them and do try to let them resolve it in their own way. If it comes to blows, then step in and take charge.

Listen to all sides, and never support one over the other in public. This can cause humiliation and foster resentment.

Promote self-respect and honor each other's opinion. All sides must be heard to lead to a resolution. Work with them to find ways to compromise.

Coaches and players work together, so why can't you?

Raising kids is not easy. You need a total team effort and, at times, an impartial referee. Enjoy the game. Go Big Blue.

How can you make sure everyone is treated the same?

Can you see how your kids think there is a rivalry? What can you do?

_____

_____

_____

_____

_____

WEEK 20 | WHAT HAPPENS IN VEGAS

WHEN SIXTH-RANKED KENTUCKY PLAYED SEVENTH-RANKED North Carolina on December 17, 2016, it was highly fitting that the game occurred amid the glitz and glamor of the Las Vegas Strip—the site of many of boxing's championship bouts. The Cats and the Heels—two heavyweight programs slugging it out—generated plenty of fisticuffs in the ring. Once again, it was powder blue versus Big Blue, the Carolina way against Calipari's way, and the Dean Dome elite clashing with the Rupp Arena faithful.

For anyone growing up in the '70s and '80s, Kentucky's biggest rival on the basketball court wasn't Duke or Indiana or Kansas or Louisville. It was, without question, the uppity University of North Carolina Tar Heels. For a couple of those decades, UK and UNC jockeyed back and forth for the distinction of being the winningest program in the history of college basketball.

Fans of the two schools were often envious of the other, always looking to outduel each other in the quest for hoops supremacy. The mere sound of Dean Smith's nasal twang, between puffs of cigarette smoke, would be enough to send bile rising from the gut of any True Blue fan. When the architect of the evil four-corners offense broke Adolph Rupp's victory record, the seeds of contempt between the two schools were permanently sown.

Big Blue Nation always travels well, and the turnout to Vegas proved no exception. On game day, T-Mobile Arena was packed with over nineteen thousand enthusiastic fans—most of them making the two-thousand-mile trek a week before Christmas clad in Kentucky blue. Throughout the week, it wasn't uncommon to hear a "Go Cats," "Go Big Blue," or "C-A-T-S" chant spontaneously erupt between yanks at the ubiquitous casino slots.

After the opening bell, the two elite hardwood programs went toe to toe. Kentucky came out swinging with a thunderous uppercut and jumped out to an early 12-point lead. Carolina responded with some lightning-quick jabs, shaving the deficit down to 56–51 at the half.

The Cats pushed the lead back out to double digits in the second stanza, only to have the pesky Tar Heels rally again. When Justin Jackson hit a three for his thirty-fourth point of the afternoon, Kentucky found itself in the unfamiliar position of trailing 100–98 with only forty-five seconds left to play.

Freshman Malik Monk then responded with what would be the biggest basket of his career. Rather than heeding the call of his coach to drive to the bucket, Monk pulled up from the right wing with a huge transition three-pointer. After a wild Carolina miss at the other end, Kentucky's De'Aaron Fox hit two free throws with 1.9 seconds left to account for the epic 103–100 Wildcat win.

After fifteen rounds, only one fighter remained standing. The Wildcats, buoyed by Malik Monk's record-setting career high of 47 points, had won the highly competitive, fast-paced game for the ages. Monk was on fire for the entire thirty-eight minutes he was on the court, hitting 18 of 28 shots from the field—including 8 of 12 three-pointers. For fans watching from the entertainment capital of the world, it was about as entertaining a game as you could ever ask for.

"If you watched that game, if you never liked basketball, you're going to start liking basketball," said Kentucky coach John Calipari. "Like, wow."

"Wow" is right. If you're a Kentucky fan, what's not to like when the Cats win big in Vegas?

PREGAME HYPE

How do you perform when the lights come on and it's showtime? When the pressure is on, are you able to pull up and hit the jump shot?

Do you lead the way and keep a cool head when your family, friends, or coworkers need you to the most? Or do you find that when the heat is on, sometimes you don't come through in the clutch?

Life is not easy, and you will often find yourself in the heat of the battle. At the same time, you want life to be fun and adventurous.

But it all depends on you and how you handle strife and tense moments.

If you stroll to your car to come home after a long day at the office and discover you have a flat tire, how do you respond? And to make matters worse, you needed to get to your child's biggest ballgame of the year, and now you might miss it altogether.

Will you keep a cool head or come out swinging and lose your temper? It's life.

THE SHOWDOWN

When you experience a difficult time or you have an intense moment meet you square in the face, the way you react says a lot about you.

You have some options: rant, snort, and scream to alleviate the tension or keep a calm demeanor and address the moment to get the win.

What are some ways you can learn to stay calm? One is to keep a journal to track how you responded to certain situations. Don't worry about what you write but focus on your emotions and how you might have handled it differently.

Take a break once in a while and leave the cares of life behind for a few hours. Spend time with family, play a round of golf, or go fishing at the local lake.

Step back and realize what is important to you and try to think of the best ways you can solve a problem.

You can also volunteer your time to help those less fortunate than you. This will help you to examine your priorities.

The best thing you can do is maintain a positive attitude. This does not mean you live in denial but that you have an optimistic outlook. When you combine this with the self-care of eating right and getting exercise and rest, you will be able to go fifteen rounds with any opponent.

Enjoy life to the fullest, and don't let a big showdown spoil your fun.

Go Big Blue!

List more ways you can stay cool under pressure.

_____

_____

_____

_____

_____

_____

WEEK 21 | THERE'S NO PLACE LIKE HOME

ON NOVEMBER 27, 1976, RICK Robey scored the first official basket in Kentucky's newly constructed Rupp Arena. On that day, with a retired Adolph Rupp among the 23,266 spectators watching from the stands, the Wildcats went on to defeat Wisconsin 72–64. Over the next four and a half decades, passionate Kentucky fans would continue to pack their iconic home venue, setting all sorts of attendance records in the process.

The all-time largest crowd to witness a Kentucky game at Rupp Arena gathered on January 2, 2010. On that day, 24,479 screaming patrons packed into Rupp to watch their beloved Wildcats take down Rick Pitino and the Louisville Cardinals 71–62. If you were lucky enough to make it through the turnstiles, you saw DeMarcus Cousins score 18 points and pull down 18 rebounds to lead the Cats to victory.

There have been many other victories in Rupp Arena. In fact, Kentucky has won over 90 percent of their games played there. It's called a home court advantage for a reason, and attendance by Kentucky fans is a big factor. Numbers don't lie. Prior to the COVID-19 pandemic, BBN led the nation in average home attendance in twenty of the last twenty-four seasons. In the years they were bumped from the top spot, they still finished a highly respectable number two.

Although large in number, Kentucky crowds at Rupp have been accused of being a bit docile. For a ho-hum, midweek game in December, that's absolutely true. You can often hear a pin drop. But bring in a big-name, blue-blooded archrival on a Saturday afternoon, and you'll see Rupp take on a life of its own—suffocating the opposition in a morass of mayhem, bedlam, and chaos.

For citizens of BBN, experiences in Rupp are like incremental rites of passage—watershed moments that define who you are and where you've been. John Wall's first-game heroics against Miami of Ohio and Anthony Davis's game-saving block against North Carolina are remembered as vividly as your wedding day or the birth of your first child.

Where were you sitting when Tayshaun hit those five consecutive threes? Or how about when the "Unforgettables" outhustled and outgunned Shaq, Chris Jackson, and Stanley Roberts in that monumental 100–95 upset of LSU? Many claim those moments as the loudest that Rupp has ever been.

Some will point to the afternoon of March 1, 1981, as the loudest moment ever. The Senior Day contest pitted ninth-ranked Kentucky against a second-ranked LSU squad looking to complete an undefeated conference slate. The Dirk Minniefield to Sam Bowie half-court alley-oop pass and dunk nearly blew the roof off the building as Kentucky pulled off the 73–71 upset victory.

Just recently, Rupp Arena got a much-needed facelift. Chair-back seating was installed in the upper-sideline areas. Because of that, and the addition of three club seating areas backstage, total courtside capacity has been cut back to 20,545.

It's a bit cozier now and a bit more confined, so it's likely we won't see many more attendance records set. But it's still home for the greatest tradition in the history of college basketball.

And for Wildcat fans who are lucky enough to have tickets, there's still no place like home.

HOME COURT ADVANTAGE

Many people live life without reason or ambition. They want to go through the motions and hope for a win. With a mundane attitude, it's easy to fit in and be a spectator.

But the happiest people are those who are focused and passionate about something.

Are you glad to just sit in the new seats, or do you have a desire to hit the winning bucket?

Do you have high ambition and want to be the best? You don't have to set the world on fire or hit five three-pointers in a row. But is there something you are passionate about?

WIN ONE FOR BBN

You can set records. You can enjoy being home and hearing the roar of the home court. You don't have to leave town to be a success.

Life is not about the constant rush and the lights and cameras of the press conference. If you want to find your passion in life, slow down the tempo and gain a better perspective of who you are as a person.

It's easier to find the answers when you step back and call a time-out.

You are the coach. Don't blame your failures on others. Own up to your mistakes and strive to become a better person.

Identify your strengths and weaknesses. Capitalize on your skills and talents. Explore what you enjoy and make a run at the basket.

At times, you need to let go of your inhibitions and take a chance. This will fuel your passion and guide your life.

Have confidence in your abilities without being cocky. Believe in your abilities and your own unique personality.

Be yourself, and don't try to live up to anyone else's expectations.

Respect your limitations, but don't be afraid to take risks. When something feels right and it works, stick with it as long as you can. Don't overthink things and remember to relax and have fun in life.

Find a friend or partner to confide in and share your experiences and dreams with.

Successful people, both in business and in life, follow their hearts.

Find your passion, and never let it go.

Go Big Blue!

What are you passionate about?

_____

_____

_____

_____

_____

_____

_____

_____

_____

_____

_____

_____

WEEK 22 | THERE WAS NO PLACE LIKE MEMORIAL COLISEUM

YOU TALK ABOUT A HOME court advantage—Kentucky had a definite advantage in Memorial Coliseum. The building known reverently as "the house that Rupp built" was home to 307 total wins versus only 38 losses. Seven of UK's teams playing in Memorial Coliseum from 1950 through 1976 posted unbeaten records, and two of those teams won NCAA titles.

The Cats won their first forty-five games in Memorial Coliseum, part of the record-setting 129-game home winning streak that will most likely stand for all eternity. The "Fiddlin' Five" played in Memorial, as did "Rupp's Runts." As such, the facility dedicated to Kentuckians who died during World War II and the Korean War is also remembered as the setting for some of the best all-star performances by many of the greatest Wildcat stars of the past.

Bill Spivey, Cliff Hagan, Frank Ramsey, Lou Tsioropoulos, Billy Evans, Bob Burrow, Johnny Cox, Cotton Nash, Louie Dampier, Pat Riley, and Dan Issel all played in Memorial Coliseum. It's a virtual pantheon of outstanding performances and seminal moments. If you had to pick one of the most memorable, however, it just might be Vernon Hatton's heroics against the Temple Owls.

The date was December 7, 1957—a date that will live in infamy. Vernon Hatton, a 6'3" senior guard out of Lafayette High School in Lexington, gave the 12,300 fans in Memorial Coliseum their absolute money's worth. With Kentucky trailing by 2, it was Hatton who hit two pressure-packed free throws to send the game into overtime.

Then, in the first overtime period, Guy Rodgers of Temple hit a jumper with three seconds to go to give the Owls another 2-point lead. After a Kentucky time-out, John Crigler inbounded the ball to Hatton, whose forty-seven-foot desperation heave somehow found the bottom of the net, sending the game into a second overtime. After the game ended, a nail was driven into the Coliseum floorboards at the exact spot where Hatton let 'er fly.

"They put in a new floor several years later," Hatton later recounted. "They cut that part of the floor with the nail out, framed it, and gave it to me. The darn thing's so heavy. If I put it on a wall, it'll tear the drywall off the wall. I don't know what I'm going to do with it."

It would take three overtimes that evening to finally settle the score. For good measure, Hatton scored the last 6 points to secure UK's 85–83 win.

That mystical 1957–1958 season was known as the year of the "Fiddlin' Five." On March 22, 1958, Ed Beck, Johnny Cox, Adrian Smith, John Crigler, and Vernon Hatton defeated Elgin Baylor and Seattle 84–72 in the NCAA title game at Louisville's Freedom Hall. It was Adolph Rupp's fourth national championship. Rupp claimed his team kept "fiddlin' around and fiddlin' around [and] then finally pulling it out at the end." The endearing nickname has stuck ever since.

The last game Kentucky played in Memorial Coliseum resulted in perhaps even more drama than the "Fiddlin' Five" could muster. On March 8, 1976, against Mississippi State, it looked as if the Cats had run out of lives. The Bulldogs, behind Ray

White's 24 points, were poised to end Kentucky's magical run in Memorial by doing the unthinkable—sending the Wildcats off on a losing note. Fortunately for Cat fans, Jack Givens keyed a late rally to snatch victory from the jaws of defeat as Kentucky escaped with a mind-numbing 94–93 overtime victory.

Wildcat fans everywhere breathed a big sigh of relief. There was no place like Memorial Coliseum. With a bucketload of glory as part of its history, there's simply no way the basketball gods were going to let Kentucky lose.

COMING OFF THE ROAD

How do you want to be remembered? You don't have to be old to think about your legacy. In fact, if you wait too long to start considering it, you might be too late.

You want your home coliseum to be one of victory and fun. You don't want your kids to long for the day that they can move out and start a new life. You want them to cherish their memories of growing up in your stadium. You want them to leave on good terms.

There are always setbacks along the way but do your best to make sure that the good memories outweigh the bad.

You have a limited amount of time to take your best shots. Make them count.

NO PLACE LIKE HOME

Your children watch the way you live more than anyone, and it's important that you live a life of integrity in front of them.

Unlike a basketball game, you have no idea how long you will be on the court of life. Live with determination that honors your creator. People will remember how you live more than your accomplishments.

Enjoy each day and push negative thoughts aside. This doesn't mean to ignore problems, but instead focus on your blessings. Love your spouse with all your heart and be dedicated to your children and family.

Keep a journal or a record of your life. It doesn't have to win a writing award, but it will allow you to reflect on your life and remind you how you handled situations.

Share your stories with your family. You can do this at dinnertime or during special weekend trips.

Be honest and authentic. Share your successes and failures, and always be transparent.

Ground your purpose to a greater cause and set the right example with your actions. Put others first and dedicate time to your children. After-hours business meetings can wait if your child has a ballgame or an event after school.

Service in your community is important. Give back and be selfless.

Share with your children what kind of lives you want them to live. Be the example.

Do you want your children to live the way you did?

When they move into their new arena, they will have the banners you have won ready to raise to the rafters.

Go Big Blue!

What can you do to promote a positive and lasting legacy? How will you be remembered in your house?

_____

_____

_____

_____

WEEK 23 | THE UNIVERSITY OF JODIE MEEKS

"WE ARE NOT THE UNIVERSITY of Jodie Meeks."

Those were the infamous words spoken by Coach Billy Gillispie regarding his talented shooting guard Jodie Meeks.

The 6'4" scoring machine out of Norcross, Georgia, had been on a tear. Point totals of 39, 37, and 46 had recently lined his ever-expanding stat sheet. Recruited by Tubby Smith, the Atlanta Player of the Year was understandably getting a healthy dose of media recognition. Gillispie, in perhaps a misguided attempt to refocus attention back on the team, uttered the words that would hasten his eventual demise.

On January 13, 2009, on a Tuesday-night ESPN telecast, Meeks went off on the University of Tennessee. Firing on all cylinders, Meeks scored 54 points, breaking the UK single game scoring record of 53 previously held by Dan Issel. Meeks put on a clinic, scorching the nets in front of 20,474 gawking onlookers at Thompson-Boling Arena. On that night, he shot 15 for 22 from the field, including 10 of 15 three-pointers. Meeks was a perfect 14–14 from the foul line, grabbed 8 rebounds, dished out 4 assists, and had 1 steal. Not a bad night's effort as Kentucky upset the twenty-fourth-ranked Vols 90–72.

UK fans remember that the game was closer than the final score indicated. With six minutes left, Tennessee had cut a comfortable 16-point Kentucky lead down to 71–64. As if on cue, Meeks immediately swished his ninth three-pointer of the game to push the lead back out to double digits. On the very next possession, Meeks picked off a pass and buried a step back NBA-length three from the right wing. His tenth bomb from behind the arc broke the record of 9 three-pointers in a game, which he had previously shared with Tony Delk. To cap off the sequence, Meeks was fouled on a three-point attempt on Kentucky's next possession and hit all 3 free throws to extend the lead back to 16.

"I was just trying to play to win," Meeks said when asked about the record-breaking performance. "I was more concerned with Tennessee trying to make a run and doing anything I could to help my teammates and get a win. It just so happened it was me that made big shots. I had a couple inches of space, so I kept shooting and they went in."

Meeks decided to forgo his senior season at UK and was selected number forty-one overall in the second round of the 2009 NBA draft by the Milwaukee Bucks. He's gone on to have a highly successful and extended professional career.

As Kentucky was clanking shots off the rim during their disappointing loss to West Virginia in the 2010 NCAA regional finals, Cat fans couldn't help but wonder what a difference Jodie Meeks would have made. If he had stuck around for his senior season, the University of Jodie Meeks could have certainly captured another elusive NCAA crown.

SCORCH THE NETS

Under every circumstance, you should always give your best effort.

Your performance might garner headlines and help you lead your family team to success. But even if you lose, you can still rest at night with a clear conscience knowing that you gave it your all.

At the same time, a good performance sometimes brings out the naysayers and jealousy from those you mistakenly thought were your supporters.

Has this ever happened to you?

Perhaps you were recognized for your hard work and diligent preparation for a project at work, and your colleagues were envious and took issue with you receiving all the credit.

Meeks set the bar at UK for his scoring ability, but the coach thought the attention he was given took away from the team.

Gillispie's attempt to draw the attention back to the team made him look petty and jealous.

In the game of life, you will win and lose. You will have moments of great triumph and some of bitter defeat.

SHARE THE SPOTLIGHT

There are times when you should receive recognition for a job well done. But a great team player, even though they deserve the credit, will always deflect the credit back to their support team.

You might have spent hours working on a big contract proposal, and you pull off the win in the end. That's a great feeling and should be rewarded. But, at the same time, you should always share the credit with those around you.

This can be done easily, and it will make those around you feel good too. Thank them on social media and bring flowers to work. Take your coworkers out to lunch, or surprise your spouse with dinner to thank them for their support during your hours away from home.

The point here is to share the spotlight. It encourages unity and promotes teamwork.

And remember to never take credit for something you did not do. The last thing you want to cause is a division between you and your peers or family.

Instead of spending a big bonus on a boat that you will one day sell, treat those around you to an appreciation party or donate to a worthy cause.

Avoid the appearance of arrogance and show gratitude. There is nothing wrong with success and getting the headlines when deserved, but you should be willing to share the spotlight with those who have also worked hard on the court or have labored behind the scenes.

The spotlight can become hot sooner or later, so make sure you have people surrounding you to keep you cool and grounded.

BBN!

Do you see the benefits of passing along the congratulations?

How can you thank others and include them in the recognition after a big win?

_____

_____

_____

_____

_____

_____

_____

_____

_____

_____

_____

WEEK 24 | ROCK-BOTTOM

SOMETIMES YOU HAVE TO HIT rock-bottom before climbing back out of the hole. For Kentucky Wildcat Basketball fans, many would claim the Billy Gillispie era as certifiably rock-bottom.

There was speculation that Billy G. was in way over his head the minute he stepped on the UK campus. Sure, he had had previous success on the basketball court. A nice run in the NCAA tournament with Texas A&M—including a win over Louisville in Rupp Arena—had made Gillispie something of a hot commodity in Lexington after Tubby Smith bolted for Minnesota. But just because you know your Xs and Os doesn't mean you can handle the pressures of being the head man at Kentucky.

In only two short years, Billy G. took Kentucky from the penthouse to the outhouse. Embarrassing home losses to Gardner Webb and VMI notwithstanding, it was his inability to handle the day-to-day rigors of running the "Roman empire" that eventually got him fired. He won forty games in his abbreviated tenure, but the awkward interviews, player abuse allegations, and rumors of hot tub escapades just couldn't be ignored.

The beginning of the end for Billy G. occurred on January 27, 2009. Kentucky, ranked twenty-fourth in the country, had gotten off to a nice 5–0 start in the SEC. They were leading Ole Miss

39–37 at the Tad Pad in Oxford when Gillispie appeared for his obligatory halftime comments in front of the ESPN cameras.

Courtside reporter Jeannine Edwards asked the UK coach about making some adjustments for Jodie Meeks—the Wildcats' top scorer—who was held to only 6 points in the first half. After emphasizing that Kentucky was not a one-man team, Billy G. condescendingly blurted out to Edwards, "What difference does it make? That's a really bad question."

No, Billy, that was a *really bad answer!* In fact, it showed the side of Billy G. that eventually got him canned. He was impulsive, quick-tempered, and overly defensive. He didn't like dealing with the media or the public. If he had his druthers, he'd just sit in his office all day and watch film. That's okay if you're coaching your local high school team, but it's totally unacceptable as the head coach of the University of Kentucky.

Kentucky went on that evening to lose to Ole Miss 85–80. They would finish the season losing ten out of their next sixteen games while missing the NCAA tournament altogether. A 77–67 NIT loss to Notre Dame put a merciful end to Gillispie's reign of terror. On the day he was fired, Gillispie was literally chased down the hallway by LEX18 reporter Alan Cutler in an attempt to get him to comment.

As bizarre as all that sounds, you can't pin all the blame on Billy. Without the proper training and support, he was put in a position where he was bound to fail. Since he left Kentucky, the poor guy has also struggled mightily with the bottle and battled some very serious health complications as well. Despite the fact that Gillispie sued UK for $6 million in an attempt to recoup his lost salary, it might be time for Kentucky fans to finally turn the other cheek. A bad hire from the get-go, Gillispie deserves at least a tiny dose of sympathy together with a generous serving of compassion.

Because of Billy Gillispie, Kentucky hit rock-bottom. And without rock-bottom, there would be no subsequent rise to the summit.

BIG RECRUITING CLASS

If you have not experienced a crushing defeat, you will. That's not to be negative or pessimistic, but no team, or person, goes through a game, or life, unscathed.

Disappointment can come in many ways. A job loss. A bad relationship. Health issues. A wayward child. Death of a loved one. Criminal activity. Drug and alcohol abuse.

The avalanche can pick up momentum quickly and engulf you before you know what has happened.

You can also get in over your head in ways that might enhance your already tense situation.

If life has a full-court press on you, there are some things you can do to beat it.

Kentucky got rid of its problem by firing Billy G.

CLIMB THE RANKINGS

Some people let the player with the ball drive to the hole to dunk it over and over again. The defense never learns.

But you can and must take charge.

The first thing you must do is recognize what has happened and feel the pain of the loss. If you try to blot it out, hitting rock-bottom has won.

You don't have to like what took place, but you must accept it and use the pain or embarrassment as motivation.

Own up to your mistakes and take responsibility. Don't pass the buck or make excuses. The bitter pill of defeat does not taste good going down, but it will make you better for the next game.

It might not hurt to share your story with a professional or a friend and vent your frustration regarding your circumstances.

You might need to adjust your attitude and demonstrate gratitude and humility. Pride can be a stubborn opponent, and it does not like to lose.

Recognize the fact that you messed up, apologize, and seek forgiveness. Be determined not to have a repeat at the next game and be ready for a long practice session.

There is no joy in hitting rock-bottom. But it's not the end of the world. You can recover.

Learn from your mistakes and get back on the court ready to play hard. You might have to win over your teammates before they trust you again or give you a second chance. Prove to them you are worth the effort and be determined to come though when the pressure is on.

Losing is not fun, but work hard to overcome the obstacles, and focus every day on the goal of hanging a victory banner in the rafters.

What lessons have you learned about hitting rock-bottom?

How can you come back?

WEEK 25 | MERCY!

THERE SHOULD BE A MERCY rule for basketball. Just ask UCLA. Yes, those same Bruins considered the "gold standard" for college basketball in the 1960s and 1970s. The same John Wooden–coached Bruins who won ten national championships in a twelve-year period. The same Bruins who were destroyed, embarrassed, and humiliated by Kentucky in the 2014 CBS Sports Classic in Chicago.

The date was December 20, 2014. Number-one-ranked Kentucky was taking on a UCLA team that—although unranked—was not devoid of talent. Granted, Lew Alcindor, Lynn Shackelford, Curtis Rowe, and Henry Bibby were not walking through that door, but potential first-round NBA draft picks Norman Powell and Kevon Looney weren't chopped liver either.

Immediately after the opening tip, you knew this one was a mismatch made in Big Blue heaven. Not only did Kentucky score the first 24 points of the game, but they also made the Bruins look like a rapidly assembled YMCA club. UCLA missed its first 17 shots from the field. Yes—17 in a row! In the first twenty minutes, the Wildcats had twice as many blocks (8) as UCLA had field goals (3).

Believe it or not, the game wasn't as close as the unbelievable 41–7 halftime score indicated. For longtime Wildcat Basketball loyalists, given the quality of the opponent and their blue-blooded pedigree, it was arguably the most dominating twenty minutes in the history of the program.

The second half was just a matter of playing out the string. Still, Kentucky extended the lead to 44 points before settling for the 83–42 blowout victory. For the game, UCLA made only 19 of 71 shots from the field. Their 7 first-half points were the fewest in school history. Freshman guard Devin Booker led the Kentucky rout with 18 points on 7 of 10 shooting (5 of 6 three-pointers).

If national championships are indeed the gold standard by which a program is judged, then UCLA still has to be considered the leader of the pack. The Bruins claim eleven titles as part of their glorious history. Kentucky checks in at number two with eight banners of their own. That disparity shrinks even more if the outcome of the 1975 championship game between the two programs was reversed. That was the game where John Wooden pulled a slick one by announcing his impending retirement the day before the tip. With everyone—including the officials—cheering for the Wizard of Westwood to ride off into the sunset with a win, Kentucky never really stood a chance.

In the 41-point blowout of the Bruins in 2014, UCLA never stood a chance. Although an early-season game in a made-for-television holiday event doesn't match the importance of a championship tilt, the carnage that day remains just as memorable in the minds of BBN.

They should have implemented the mercy rule.

IN THE HUDDLE

Like most people, you have probably experienced both ends of the spectrum. You were either blown off the field by your opponent or you were the one doing the blowing out. In either situation, not much is learned when this happens.

The team being run over grows discouraged, while the unit in control loses its sense of competition and slacks off in performance.

Nothing really good comes out of it except for a W for one squad and demoralization for the other.

And sometimes there's nothing you can do but wait for the clock to wind down.

Life has its blowouts too. You might have a few bad days where nothing goes right. The best attitude and approach in these cases is to keep going but find a way to change up the routine a little.

Don't lose focus or allow a thumping to detract from your mission.

SPORTSMANSHIP

When life is beating you down, it's easy to give up.

But if you do, then you do an injustice to yourself and to those who love and support you.

Keep in mind that everyone goes through valleys in life. The climb to the top only makes the view better when you reach the summit.

For some, the journey doesn't take long. And for others, like you, it might go into overtime.

Life is meant to be enjoyed. This doesn't mean you won't encounter struggles. But for the most part, focus on the positive, and demonstrate good sportsmanship.

You know how it feels when someone runs up the score on you. It's not fun. Vengeance is not a motivator.

You can apply the same principles in life as in sports.

Avoid arguing and taunting.

Play fair, even if others around you don't. Sinking to a level below your expectations is never the solution.

Follow directions. Without rules, there is chaos.

Whether your team loses or wins, show respect to all involved.

Honor decisions made by the "officials" in your life. This can be your spouse or employers or anyone who might be joined with you in life or in business. This also goes for sports your children might be involved with. Don't be "that parent" who always questions the calls.

Be agreeable yet stern. Never let anyone walk all over you or take you for granted.

When you extend mercy and sportsmanship to others, you expect that it will be returned to you. But that's not always the case. Extend it anyway.

Be the bigger person in life.

Have mercy.

Go Cats.

How can you show compassion to others?

_____

_____

_____

_____

_____

_____

_____

_____

_____

WEEK 26 | MERCY ME!

IF THERE ARE KENTUCKY BASKETBALL blowout games that should have invoked the mercy rule, there's one Kentucky Basketball *play* that qualifies for inclusion on that list.

It happened on Saturday, March 21, 2015, in the third round of the NCAA Midwest regional in Louisville, Kentucky. The top-seeded and undefeated Wildcats were facing off against the unranked Cincinnati Bearcats for the right to advance to the regional semifinals.

Coming into the contest, Kentucky was on a collision course with history, attempting to become the first unbeaten team since the 1976 Indiana Hoosiers to win an NCAA championship. The team had blitzed through the regular season with a couple of close calls but had emerged into the tournament with nary a blemish on their record.

Just a couple of nights earlier, heavily favored Kentucky had routinely dispatched the Hampton University Pirates by a 79–56 score to win their opening-round game. Against the undermanned Bearcats on this particular afternoon, however, a rather sluggish start had the partisan blue crowd in the YUM Center slightly agitated. The Wildcats actually trailed by a score of 24–23 when Willie Cauley-Stein committed a crime against humanity.

Kentucky's junior center's vicious rim-rattling dunk not only helped stake the Cats to a 31–24 halftime lead; it also sent the hapless Cincinnati defender sprawling helplessly onto the court. After he was posterized on the play, the Bearcats' Quadri Moore allegedly entered witness protection. His teammate, Octavius Ellis, also disappeared with a back injury as part of the collateral damage. Reports from on high indicated that neither player was ever the same.

Kentucky went on cruise control in the second half for a rather mundane 64–51 victory. Aaron Harrison led the Wildcats that night with a 13-point effort. Trey Lyles chipped in with 11 points and 11 rebounds. But everyone in the arena knew that the game ended in the first half when Willie threw down the most memorable soul-shattering dunk in the history of the program.

Willie Cauley-Stein was one of a kind. The seven-footer from Spearville, Kansas, played football for Olathe Northwest High School (bet you didn't know he played wide receiver). Whether riding around the UK campus on a scooter, dyeing his hair blond, or coloring in his books, WCS remains not only a Renaissance man of the highest blue order but one of the best dunkers in UK Basketball history. If you see him coming down the lane, you better just get out of the way.

Willie earned First Team All-American and First Team All-SEC honors during his time at Kentucky. He was also voted the 2015 SEC Defensive Player of the Year. After his junior season, Willie declared early for the NBA draft and was selected number six overall in the first round by the Sacramento Kings.

His professional career thus far has been a bit less than stellar, but for Big Blue fans everywhere, Willie Cauley-Stein's dunk against Cincinnati will remain forever Hall of Fame worthy.

TRAILING BY ONE

Marching to the beat of your own drum is fine as long as you continue to show respect for your parents, children, and authority figures in your life.

Rules are made to be followed, but at times they can be bent.

If you are a nonconformist, you may not necessarily be a rebel, but you may gain a reputation of always going against the grain with no room for compromise.

Perhaps you have tried other ways and feel more comfortable with your own style.

Or maybe in the past, people on the job, at school, or even in your own home have tried to walk all over you.

Have there been times in your past when you should have been out in front, but for some unexplained reason, you were behind by a few points?

You need to make a thunderous dunk to get back in the game and give momentum to yourself and to your team.

RATTLE THE RIM

Being bold and confident does not always mean being arrogant.

There are times when you need to make it clear that you are serious and a force to be reckoned with. It's important that you do not let your opponent see you sweat or become impatient.

Capitalize on the opportunity to fend off your defenders and pound the ball through the rim, and you might inspire others to do the same.

The play could grab the attention of others and send a message, or it could be part of a subtle game plan.

When you make a mistake, the way you respond to it can be an encouragement to others. Shake it off, get back on the court, and determine not to let it happen again. When others mess up, lift them up and reassure them it will be okay.

Celebrate the small things others do as well as the ginormous dunks that grab all the headlines.

Motivate others by recognizing their accomplishments, big or small. Reward your children for doing the little things you ask them to do.

You can make a big play just by listening. When you let others know you care enough to hear them, that is just as groundbreaking as a tomahawk jam.

Make it a priority to accomplish your goals daily or at least weekly. You might have to make a checklist or put a reminder in your phone to remember a special occasion. What may not be a priority to you might be critical to your spouse, parents, or family.

Just showing up at an event or lending a hand can give your team members the boost they need.

And always be confident in your abilities. Adopt a mindset that prompts you to seek advice and ask questions.

Wisdom is a wonderful tool that can lead you to make the big dunk you need in life.

When you put all this together, you can inspire others around you and encourage them to walk to their own beat. You can be the one who slams the ball home at the right time.

Go Big Blue!

What are some ways you can promote self-confidence in others around you and encourage them to make the big play?

_____

_____

_____

_____

_____

_____

_____

_____

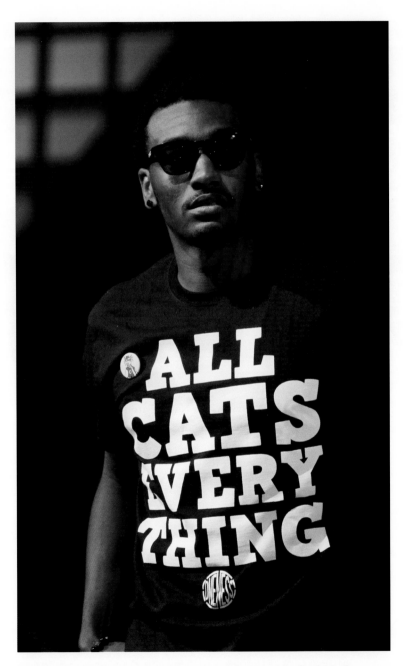

John Wall, who changed the perception of the Kentucky basketball
program in 2010, is one "cool" Cat. *All photo credits: Dr. Michael Huang*

Wildcats celebrate a big 76–69 win over North Carolina
on their way to the 2011 NCAA Final Four.

DeAndre Liggins was a defensive stopper against the higher-seeded Tar Heels, a team that boasted the likes of future NBA stars Harrison Barnes, Tyler Zeller, and John Henson.

Coach John Calipari's famous embrace of DeAndre Liggins after Liggins hit the dagger three-pointer that cemented the win over Carolina.

The "University of Jodie Meeks" was an institution of higher scoring.

Brandon Knight with the game-winning layup versus Princeton, saving the Wildcats from an early exit in the first round of the 2011 NCAA tournament.

Aaron Harrison was 3–0 versus Louisville during his career—including the huge 74–69 win in the Sweet Sixteen round of the 2014 NCAA tournament.

Malik Monk hangs 47 points on North Carolina as Kentucky defeats the Tar Heels 103–100 in an epic battle on the Las Vegas Strip.

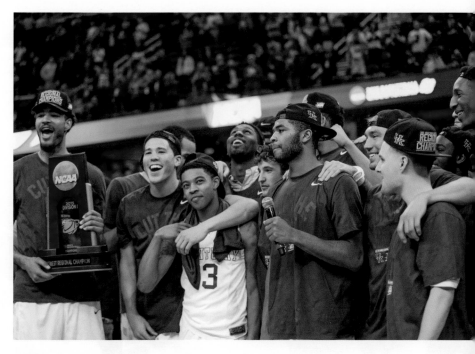

Wildcats celebrate the Midwest regional championship
on their way to the 2015 NCAA Final Four.

Julius Randle and Andrew Harrison surrounded by "Kentucky Passion" after the Wildcats' thrilling 77–76 OT victory over LSU.

Willie Cauley-Stein and Marcus Lee celebrating Wildcats' 75–72 win over Michigan in the 2014 Midwest regional finals in Indianapolis.

Karl Anthony-Towns averaged 10.3 points and 6.7
rebounds on the 2015 Wildcat team that went 38–1.

Above, Nerlens Noel holds the UK single-game record for the most blocked shots with 12.

Facing, "KAT" was unstoppable in Kentucky's 68–66 victory over Notre Dame in the regional final, scoring 25 points on 10 of 13 shooting.

View from the eRUPPtion Zone student section
of another sold-out Rupp Arena.

Rupp Arena, which opened in 1976, allowed Kentucky
to lead the nation in average home attendance in twenty
of the last twenty-four seasons (prior to 2020).

Like many first-round NBA draft picks, for "Bam" Adebayo,
the road to family riches runs directly through Lexington.

Another SEC tournament championship celebration
for the 2015–2016 Wildcats.

Aaron Harrison's game-winning three versus Wisconsin in the semifinals of the 2014 Final Four—"This is the point where he always hits it."

Jack "Goose" Givens and his 41-point performance against Duke in the
1978 NCAA championship game will always be remembered by BBN.

Dan Issel, UK's all-time leading scorer in basketball, with Benny Snell Jr., UK's all-time leading rusher in football, attending a recent game at Rupp Arena.

Tayshaun Prince acknowledges the crowd in his return to
Rupp Arena, site of his five consecutive three-point shots to
begin the game versus North Carolina back in 2001.

Nick Richards, Ashton Hagans, and Tyrese Maxey do their victory dance after beating archrival Louisville.

Swish!

Mercy me—Willie Cauley-Stein with a crime against humanity!

CONFERENCE GRIND

WEEK 27 | COOL CATS

JOHN WALL FOREVER CHANGED THE perception of Kentucky Basketball. When he and DeMarcus Cousins signed on to play for the Wildcats in 2009, Kentucky suddenly became the team to cheer for. Prior to that, the program with the greatest tradition in the history of college basketball was just that—traditional, old school, and a bit on the stodgy side. That all changed when John Wall did the John Wall Dance at Big Blue Madness on Friday, October 16, 2009. The script was flipped, and Kentucky became the cool school.

On November 16, 2009, the 6'4" point guard from Word of God Christian Academy in Raleigh, North Carolina, made quite the splashy Rupp Arena debut. His twelve-foot step back jump shot from the left wing with just half a tick left on the clock gave Kentucky a heart-pounding 72–70 victory over Miami (Ohio). Right from the get-go, Kentucky fans knew they had something unique and incredibly special.

Together with DeMarcus "Boogie" Cousins, the big 6'11" teddy bear of a center from Mobile, Alabama, Kentucky would finish out the season with a sparkling thirty-five-win slate. Throughout the campaign, Cousins endeared himself to the UK fan base not only with his masterful skills in the paint but also with his fun-loving antics toward opposing crowds. Who can forget his "call me" hand gesture to the Mississippi State student body after his rebound and dunk off a missed shot? If you remember, the day before, Bulldog fans had gotten ahold of DeMarcus's phone number and bombarded him with an avalanche of pesky text messages and phone calls.

Another memorable phone call occurred when President Barack Obama dialed in to congratulate the team for their participation in the Haiti earthquake relief efforts. Boogie's "Hello, Mr. President. This is DeMarcus Cousins" greeting remains a classic UK soundbite.

Are we having fun yet? Here's another memorable moment that will make all UK fans smile.

It's March 14, 2010, and Kentucky is playing Mississippi State in the SEC tournament championship game. As usual, the blue mist has descended into Bridgestone Arena in Nashville. The 20,082 mostly Kentucky fans are on the edge of their seats as Mississippi State grabs a 64–61 lead with only 8.2 seconds to go. After Eric Bledsoe intentionally misses the second of two free throws, Patrick Patterson tips the ball to the right corner where Wall tracks it down, shakes his man, and fires up a desperation shot that barely nicks the rim. Cousins grabs the near air ball, lays it in, and ties the game at the buzzer.

The ensuing celebration begins with Wall and Cousins sprinting down to the other end of the court . . . and ends with Wall tackling Cousins to initiate the ceremonial dog pile. In overtime, Kentucky wasn't to be denied. Appropriately, Wall hits a three with 22.6 seconds to go, and Cousins seals the deal with a free throw with 5.3 seconds remaining to give Kentucky the 75–74 overtime win.

"You know what, they've been doing it all year," UK coach John Calipari said afterward. "They have an unbelievable will to win."

They're also a couple of really cool Cats.

PREGAME JITTERS

Have you always done something the same way because that's how it's always been done? Before 2009, Kentucky Basketball was always respected and feared, but until John Wall came on to the scene, they had never been regarded as "cool."

His attitude and enthusiasm changed fans' perception of the team.

Do you find yourself in a similar circumstance? Maybe you are in a rut and need a positive change of pace.

Perhaps some don't take you as seriously as you would like, or your accomplishments have been overlooked in both your professional and personal life.

Maybe you need to spruce up your reputation.

PLAYER INTRODUCTIONS

It's never too late to bring about motivational changes in your life and add some fun and excitement to your daily routine.

There are ways to stand out and earn the respect and admiration of others.

Give more. Donate to charities and worthy causes and volunteer your time. Help a friend at work with a project, blow the dust off your honey-do list, and spend quality time with your kids.

Smile more. A smile can be contagious. Many players and fans liked to be around John Wall because he made them feel good. You may not be able to dance like him, but you can shine a bright light of hope on others with your smile and laughter.

When you take time to help someone in need or send a thank-you card or email, you are sending a message that the other person is important.

Always be honest with your family and your coworkers, even if it leads to negative consequences. Be willing to take the heat when you make a bad decision, and then put yourself in the position to make a run to hit the winner at the buzzer.

Being popular doesn't mean you are always right, but it should inspire you to do the right thing when you know others are watching. Honesty is always cool.

Do things for others that also make you feel good about yourself.

Engage in random acts of kindness. Pay for the coffee of someone in line behind you. Or surprise your spouse with a weekend getaway. It's not about you; it's about you doing something awesome for someone who is important to you.

Take a day just to spend with your kids or visit a friend who is ill or discouraged.

When you put others first, you become the cool kid on the block.

Go Cats!

How can you be considered cool?

_____

_____

_____

_____

_____

_____

_____

_____

_____

WEEK 28 | THE RED MENACE

IN THE BATTLE FOR COLLEGE basketball supremacy in the '70s, UK's biggest rival was the University of North Carolina. But their most *intense* rivalry was actually with the red menace from the border state up north—the Indiana Hoosiers. Anyone with blue coursing through their veins remembers all the injustices heaped on BBN by the team with the candy-striped warm-up pants. Who can forget the likes of Kent Benson and his luckier-than-dirt game-winning tip-in, or Bobby Knight's affectionate love tap to the back of Joe Hall's head, or Steve Alford's perfect hair, or Damon Bailey's free throws . . . and of course the Watford shot? Before Indiana Basketball's spiral into obscurity, the Hoosiers were public enemy number one.

It's Saturday, December 7, 1974, and Kentucky is making its biannual trip up to Bloomington for the border war with Indiana. It's an already harsh rivalry that has escalated recently due to the addition of Bobby Knight, the volatile up-and-coming head coach of the Hoosiers.

This one's a mismatch, as Indiana—with All-Americans Scott May, Kent Benson, Quinn Buckner, and Steve Green—dominates the Wildcats from the outset in a 98–74 blowout victory. With the outcome firmly decided, Knight inexplicably keeps his starters on the floor well into the second half. Kentucky coach Joe B. Hall is perplexed by the move and addresses the issue with Knight during a break in the action.

"We were down by about 30, and Coach took all of the start-ers out and put the reserves in," recounted UK All-American Kevin Grevey, who chipped in with 17 points that afternoon. "Bobby Knight kept his starters. I was sitting next to Coach Hall, and I heard him ask his assistant coaches, 'How bad does he want to beat us?' Finally, they score another basket, and he looked down at Bobby Knight and said, 'Bobby, what's going on? You got us by 30, and I've got my subs in.' Knight respond-ed, 'You coach your team, and I'll coach mine, Joe.' That's when they met, and that's when the back slap happened . . . and the glasses go flying."

The infamous "back slap" between alleged fishing buddies would be the impetus that would propel that 1975 Kentucky team all the way to the NCAA championship game later that year. Along the way, they would meet up with the Hoosiers again in what many consider one of the greatest revenge perfor-mances in UK Basketball lore.

On March 22, 1975, Kentucky and Indiana are paired up again in the NCAA Mideast regional finals with the winner ad-vancing to the Final Four. A hyped-up Dayton Arena crowd of 13,458 watches as a Kentucky team that was humiliated by the stronger and quicker Hoosiers in their earlier meeting some-how finds a way to beat IU at their own game and snap IU's thirty-four-game winning streak. Kentucky forces 20 Indiana turnovers and, with their twin towers of Rick Robey and Mike Phillips doing damage inside, manages to hold off a final Indi-ana spurt for the emotional 92–90 win. Afterward, the iconic photo of Kentucky guard and Indiana native Mike Flynn—who led UK in scoring with 22 points—cutting down the nets re-mains etched in every Wildcat fan's memory banks.

Sadly, Kentucky and Indiana no longer play each other on a regular basis. But for longtime Cat fans, memories of the rivalry with the formidable red menace will live on in their hearts and minds forever.

THE BIG DEFEAT

Perhaps on the field of competition, either in the boardroom or in your personal life, someone has clobbered you. Defeat is especially hard to swallow when your opponent is not only trying hard to win but attempting to humiliate you as well.

Life can deal some harsh blows. Maybe you lose your job due to a layoff, and your boss takes the opportunity to dump on you during your final days on the payroll.

Or maybe you were up against a colleague for a promotion. Your competition wins the spot and rubs your nose in it for weeks.

Maybe you have a secret admiration for a special person and decide to ask them out for a date. You finally muster up the courage, but they not only reject you but squash any self-confidence you might have.

There are ways to rebound.

THE REMATCH

The key here is to never let your opponent see you sweat.

When confronted with a tormentor, A. Giannoccaro instructs you to "kill them with kindness, slay them with a smile and murder them with a kiss."

This is good advice. It will help you to avoid unnecessary battles and might even turn an enemy into a friend.

Never underestimate the power of kindness. When you demonstrate this in various forms in the face of those who did you wrong, you might cause them to have second thoughts, and guilt may even begin to weigh on their conscience.

Showing kindness instead of outrage puts you ahead in the game.

When you respond to cruelty with goodwill, you take away any power that your agitators may have over you.

When confrontation comes knocking, be the bigger person. When you react with gentleness and humility, you are actually winning the battle.

This might not seem the best approach in the heat of the battle, but it will bring you a win in the long run.

It's easy to respond by yelling or striking back, but that's not the wisest course of action.

When you react with a tender heart, you show virtue and character.

If your colleague flaunts success in your face, invite them to lunch. When the person who laid you off from your job has something go wrong in their life, send them a card to wish them well.

Show you are an adult.

Revenge should never be a motivating factor but showing affection and thoughtfulness toward a person who did you wrong is a great way to respond. It will drive them bananas.

Your kindness shows them that they did not win. And you are not a loser or a quitter.

Win in the end with a smile and gratitude.

Go Big Blue!

List some ways you can show kindness to someone who has tried to hurt you.

WEEK 29 | WOOOOOOOO, PIG! SOOIE!

WITH SUCH A RICH TRADITION of dominance over its SEC basketball brethren, it's hard to imagine the University of Kentucky ever being considered anything other than top dog. After all, if forty-nine regular-season championships and thirty-one tournament titles doesn't qualify you for exalted status in the league, then I'm not sure what does. Especially when you consider that the teams in second have only eleven (LSU with regular season) and six (Alabama with conference tournament) titles, respectively.

And yet, longtime Cat fans will remember when the University of Arkansas actually did challenge the Wildcats for conference supremacy. Beginning with the 1991–1992 season, Coach Nolan Richardson and his "40 minutes of Hell" pumped unparalleled excitement into the league as the new kids on the SEC block.

During that time, the Razorbacks—transplants from the Southwest Conference—not only finished first or tied for first in the conference an amazing six out of seven years, but the newcomers from Fayetteville also happened to win a national championship along the way, barely missing out on rare back-to-back titles. Plus, they did it all in a fashion that challenged Kentucky's status as king of the SEC hill. They pushed the bully to the brink, taunting BBN with a fast-paced, in-your-face brand of basketball that had Cat fans licking their wounds on a yearly basis. Throw in that "Wooooooooo, pig! Sooie!" and a cheering President Bill Clinton, and you can see why Kentucky fans felt just a bit threatened.

One particular game between the Cats and the Hogs stands head and shoulders above the rest. It went down on March 12, 1995, at the SEC tournament in Atlanta, Georgia. Occasionally referred to as the "Rodrick Rhodes meltdown game," the overtime tilt between the two highly ranked programs became an instant classic. Third-ranked Kentucky was on a tear, in search of its fourth straight SEC tournament title. But it was the fifth-ranked Razorbacks—the defending national champs—that came storming out of the gate.

Just ten minutes into the game, the Hogs led 35–16, and it looked like the blowout was on. Kentucky, however, ratcheted up the defense, hit a few key shots, and closed to within 50–44 at the half.

Arkansas, led by All-Americans Corliss Williamson and Scotty Thurman, started the second half just like they did the first—rebuilding much of their lead. But Kentucky held on by the skin of their teeth and slowly battled back to tie the score at 80 with six seconds left in regulation. Rhodes then stole the ball and was fouled. He stepped to the line for two shots with 1.3 seconds remaining for a chance to win the game and the tournament championship. He missed them both.

A despondent and tearful Rhodes then watched from the bench as Kentucky fell behind 91–82 in the overtime period. With the boisterous and jubilant Arkansas faithful "calling the hogs," the Cats mounted one final comeback. Tony Delk hit a crucial three to pull the Wildcats to within 93–90. Antoine Walker and Anthony Epps then came up with crucial steals to somehow will Kentucky to an improbable victory.

Final score: Kentucky 95, Arkansas 93.

Wheeeeeeeew! Pig! Sooie!

GET BACK IN THE GAME

Have you ever been put on the line with a lot at stake? Some challenges are more monumental than others, and your own personal obstacles might seem enormous to you.

Life sometimes includes some hard problems. Your business may be failing, or you might be facing a job loss, family issue, or health problem.

Time spent on earth might appear to be long, but in reality, it's brief and passes by before you know it.

When you see your dreams and wishes fade away, the way you respond to these disappointments depends on your frame of mind.

You can give up, accept pending defeat, and miss the free throws life gives you, or you can respond with action and meet the obstacles head-on. It's your choice.

STEP UP TO THE LINE

The pressure of the moment got the best of Rodrick Rhodes, but that did not make him less of a player. If anything, he most likely learned from his mistakes.

Very often, it's not tomorrow that scares us; it's today.

What information will that email contain about a job interview?

What do you do when you receive a text from a love interest that says, "We need to talk"?

How do you respond when your boss calls you into the office and says, "Sit down"?

Learn how to embrace uncertainty. This does not mean to expect bad things to happen, it means make a contingency plan in case your original plans don't work out.

Let go of what you envisioned and enjoy the moment you live in now. This does not mean to give up on dreams but rather to embrace the present.

Life is full of negative and positive adventures and results. Some days will be hectic, and others will be calm. If a problem is fixable, then handle it. But if you cannot, then don't force an outcome. Control what you can to the best of your ability by focusing on your attitude and effort.

Try not to take disappointments personally. Many people become depressed when a major life event catches them off guard. When you step up to the line and the pressure mounts, call time-out and evaluate what your strategy should be. Draw out the play and remember how you practiced for this moment.

Keep moving forward and understand that if you don't hit the mark this time, the sun will still rise tomorrow, and there will always be a new season. Keep fighting and develop your game plan for the future.

You will get through your challenge and be a better person in the end. You might clink your shot off the rim, or miss that pressure-packed foul shot, but you will be back on the court ready to hit the game-winner soon.

Go Big Blue!

How can you rise to the challenge?

_____

_____

_____

_____

_____

_____

_____

_____

WEEK 30 | ALL HE DOES IS WIN

REMEMBER CHUCK HAYES? IF YOU don't, that's okay; you're probably not alone. The 6'6" 242-pound workhorse of a player from Modesto, California, is frequently glossed over when perusing the list of University of Kentucky greats.

In fact, many ardent Wildcat fans can't even recall a specific Chuck Hayes breakout moment during his entire four-year college career. You'll find no last-second field goals, scoring barrages, or iconic rim-rattling dunks in this chapter. With an undersized body but an oversized heart, Hayes literally willed himself to greatness through determination, hard work, and hustle.

During Hayes's senior season, when Kentucky was promoting him as an All-American candidate, UK Athletics adopted the slogan "All He Does Is Win." In hindsight, you couldn't have come up with a more appropriate catchphrase for the man who did it all. If you needed that crucial rebound, that timely assist, or that game-saving steal, chances are that Chuck Hayes was the one to deliver.

Over Hayes's sophomore, junior, and senior seasons, Kentucky finished with an enviable 87–15 team record while being ranked first, second, and seventh in the national polls. By the time he graduated, Hayes ranked seventh individually in all-time rebounds (910), eighth in steals (169), ninth in blocked shots (128), and thirty-fifth in total career points (1,211). During his senior season, he was selected as the SEC Defensive Player of the Year. However, he never did end up making All-American, nor did he ever experience that elusive Final Four.

Chuck Hayes was a fan favorite who seemed to always be in the right place at the right time. Together with Erik Daniels, the two became one of the most prolific passing big-man combos UK fans have ever witnessed. There were times the ball zipped around the paint as if part of a Harlem Globetrotter screenplay. By the time the defender got their bearings, the ball would be halfway through the hoop.

The most amazing thing about Hayes was what happened after his UK career ended. Considered way too small to play center in the pros, he went undrafted in the 2005 NBA draft. Picked up as a free agent by the Houston Rockets, he played several games before being banished to the D League.

Injuries to key Rocket players the next year gave Hayes a second chance at making the team. In just the second day of a ten-day contract, Hayes scored 12 points and grabbed 13 rebounds in a double overtime win against Chicago. Houston signed him for the rest of the season, and, as they say, the rest is history.

Chuck Hayes went on to have a fabulous twelve-year NBA career. Along the way, he signed a four-year, $22 million deal with the Sacramento Kings in 2011 that set him up for life.

By all accounts, Hayes was too short and too slow to play center in either college or the NBA. He wasn't a great shooter, he had no hops, and he didn't excel particularly well in the transition game. What made him successful was his desire and his heart. It's absolutely true that when it came to effort and results, all the guy did was win.

AGAINST THE ODDS

Have you ever felt like you were up against an enormous wall with no way to climb over? Maybe you are facing what seems like the biggest mountain you have ever faced in your life. Your first challenge is how you approach it mentally.

Perhaps you have an assignment at work you think is unreasonable. Or maybe you are going for a job interview and are intimidated by the competition, which is stronger than you thought it was going to be.

Maybe you have dreams about the future that your friends have discouraged you from pursuing because they don't believe you can do it.

How do you respond?

Do circumstances out of your control influence your attitude? Do you give up, or do you get busy?

BREAK THE PRESS

There are ways to meet challenges for the better. Will you overcome them? Not unless you try. Never let the fear of defeat stop you. Instead, lace up your sneakers and grab the rebound.

Chuck Hayes did not allow what others perceived as physical limitations to stop him from pursuing a wonderful career in the NBA.

He got it done because of his will and determination.

If you are under pressure to meet a deadline, focus on your goal, and tune out the distractions. Turn off your phone or social media until your obligation is met.

If you lose your focus at work or at home, you lose productivity as well as valuable time that you will never get back.

Keep your eye on the eventual outcome. Remind yourself that you have to finish strong to receive the reward in store. Allow your goals to motivate you to give it your all.

Incentive is wonderful motivation.

Take your spouse out to dinner or the kids to the park as a way to reward yourself for a job well done.

Make sure you get plenty of rest and exercise to keep your stress levels down.

When you are up against the odds, maintain a positive attitude and strive for the prize. Go the extra mile in the interview and prepare a slideshow presentation that will turn into a slam dunk.

Hayes had to work harder than most players and do things that were not glamourous but were effective.

There is no replacement for hustle and grit. Put your team on the front page and be the one who consistently gets the job done right. And when the time comes, make a run at that special position you've longed for. Go back to college and obtain that degree you have wanted.

Having the heart and will to overcome the odds is the first step to reaching your goal.

What are some ways you can go the extra mile?

_____

_____

_____

_____

_____

_____

_____

WEEK 31 | NUMBER ONE AND HOLDING

TWO OF THE MOST PRESTIGIOUS University of Kentucky Basketball records may never be broken. Not so coincidentally, they're both held by Dan Issel, arguably one of the best players to ever wear the Blue and White.

From 1967 through 1970, in his three seasons with the varsity (he played before freshmen were eligible), Issel poured in 2,138 total career points and pulled down 1,078 total rebounds—both UK records. In this current age of the best college players being one-and-done players, it's doubtful you'll see anyone top those numbers anytime soon.

"I'm shocked that my scoring record still stands," Issel said recently. "Not so much now—I think now that record might stand for a while. Anybody good enough to score that many points is going to be long gone before they get to that total. But what really surprised me was that shortly after I played, the players got to play four years instead of three, and the three-point line comes along—so I'm surprised it wasn't broken early on. Now if I stayed around for four years, that means I stunk."

Kentucky fans lucky enough—and old enough—to have witnessed Issel's exploits will certainly remember his scoring duels with Pete Maravich. "Pistol Pete" was a veritable scoring machine, playing for his father, who designed the LSU offense directly around his son. In six meetings against the Wildcats, Maravich averaged a mind-boggling 52 points per game. Coach Adolph Rupp's strategy against the Tigers was always to let Pete get his points while keeping the rest of his teammates at bay. The strategy worked to perfection as the Cats never lost; they won every single game by a comfortable double-digit margin.

One of those contests took place on Saturday, February 21, 1970, in Baton Rouge. Issel led the Wildcats that day to a fast-paced, head-turning 121–105 conference win, scoring 51 points and pulling down 17 rebounds in the process. Believe it or not, "Pistol Pete" outscored Issel by 13—tallying 64 total points, all without the benefit of the three-point line. Such was life for Dan Issel back in the day. With his career running concurrently with Maravich's, Issel never led the league in scoring with his "pedestrian" 25.7 points per game average.

Neither Issel nor Maravich ever made it to the Final Four either. Issel got close on March 14, 1970, playing on one of the best Kentucky teams never to win a title. The Cats were ranked number one at the time when they suffered a heartbreaking 106–100 defeat to Artis Gilmore's Jacksonville University at the NCAA Mideast regional finals in Columbus, Ohio. With 10:16 still left to play in the game, Issel fouled out when Jacksonville's Vaughn Wedeking snuck up in front of him on the way up the court and elicited a highly questionable charging call. Shortly after Issel was disqualified, Kentucky All-Americans Mike Pratt, Larry Steele, and Terry Mills were also whistled to the sidelines with five fouls apiece.

Many old-timers will tell you Kentucky got robbed in what remains one of the most memorable losses in school history.

They'll also tell you that Dan Issel knew how to put the ball in the hole. In addition to being UK's all-time career leader in points, "The Horse" also held the single-game UK scoring record for over thirty-eight years. He scored 40 or more points nine times in his college career, and he broke the 50-point barrier twice. Although the two-time All-American went on to score more than 27,000 points in his long and distinguished career in the ABA and NBA, he's still number one in the hearts and minds of BBN for his accomplishments at UK.

STUDY THE GAME PLAN

How do your accomplishments stand up over time? Maybe you are just now beginning your stint and are a walk-on freshman in the game of life. Perhaps you have lofty goals and want to conquer the world. Or maybe the time has come for you to retire and reflect on your career.

RAISE THE BANNER

If you play hard and follow the rules, you are a great team player. You don't have to win a championship or an award to validate yourself. Showing up on the court to play your best every day is a great achievement.

Recognition for a job well done is nice, but your main focus should be on your character and reputation. After all, someone has to do the grunt work.

Put your family first. This team is your obligation and should take priority. Make sure you are always there for your spouse and children. Make sure that missing any of your children's functions is a rarity. Your employers won't be at your bedside when it comes time to turn out the lights in the gym. That boss of yours won't be knocking at your door when the shot clock expires.

Be involved in community and charity events. Volunteer your time for worthy causes and be a beacon for good in your neighborhood.

The limelight is nice, but at the end of the day, it will eventually be turned out.

Make sure you treat those close to you the best. Make an impact within your circles and set the example as a good person with character and integrity.

When you make a positive difference in the lives of those around you, you have set the bar high for others to follow.

Always keep in mind it's never too late to raise a banner in your own home or community. If you want to leave a lasting legacy, or begin one on the right note, play hard like Dan Issel. Be committed and honor your word. Compete with the best.

Be that one person who others depend on and make an impact for all to remember.

You don't have to win a scoring title or a national championship to be considered one of the best ever.

Set the tone and lead the way. Be the one who causes a smile to come across a face when you walk into a room. That is a banner everyone wants to raise.

How can you make a positive impact?

_____

_____

_____

_____

_____

_____

_____

_____

_____

WEEK 32 | PIONEER DAYS

OCCASIONALLY, YOU'LL STILL HEAR UK fans say that when Kentucky won their seventh national title in 1998 under first-year coach Tubby Smith, they did it with Pitino's players. Nothing could be further from the truth.

Although Rick didn't exactly leave the cupboard bare when he bolted for Boston, no Kentucky fan in their right mind could have anticipated another championship run with the talent left over in Lexington. Don't get me wrong—Jeff Sheppard, Allen Edwards, Cameron Mills, Scott Padgett, Wayne Turner, Nazr Mohammed, Heshimu Evans, and Jamaal Magloire were all quality players. But to think they'd be cutting down the nets in San Antonio at the end of Tubby's inaugural season was a dream that was Alamo worthy.

After an up-and-down slosh through the regular season, Kentucky entered March that year on a roll. The team blitzed through the SEC tournament on its way to a number-two seeding in the NCAA South region. South Carolina State, St. Louis, and UCLA fell easily in the first three rounds. Comeback victories against Duke and Stanford (in overtime) followed next, and the Cats surprisingly found themselves still clawing on championship night.

As far as memories are concerned—for Kentucky fans at least—Monday, March 30, 1998, remains one of the most joyful times ever. Unexpected victories make for happy surprises, and this '98 team delivered the best one of all. Down 50–40 early in the second half to the Utah Utes, the team could have easily folded. Instead, they dug deep, the Utes went cold, and the Cats ultimately prevailed with a 78–69 victory. As the final buzzer sounded, Tubby bounded exuberantly onto the court, his face a mask of pure euphoria, his arms raised triumphantly during the exhilarating victory celebration. This was his team—not Rick's—and nobody was going to steal their joy,

With few exceptions (Merlene Davis of the *Lexington Herald-Leader* being the most notable), Orlando "Tubby" Smith was a popular choice to replace Rick Pitino. He had served admirably under Rick during the early days of Camelot before going on to successful stints of his own at Tulsa and Georgia. In addition to being skilled at Xs and Os, it was Tubby's character and composure that made him the right man for the job.

Whether he liked it or not, being the first African American coach in the history of the program made Tubby a pioneer. It was a role and responsibility he took rather seriously. He knew full well about the program's underlying racial strife, and he accepted the responsibilities of being a trailblazer. As people watched his every move, Tubby made every effort to always act honorably and respectfully. He understood that any slip-ups along the way could be used against other African American coaches who were trying to move up the corporate coaching ladder.

Although championship number seven was nothing to scoff at, what Tubby Smith did during those pioneer days at Kentucky will forever remain the biggest part of his legacy. Under the circumstances of the moment and the constant pressure to win, he always managed to act with grace, dignity, and class. During his ten-year stint, he represented his race, his university, and the commonwealth of Kentucky in an exemplary fashion. In hindsight, that's every bit as joyful as the championship he earned on the basketball court.

GAME FILM SESSION

You might be in a position where you are taking over someone's role at work or even at home. Perhaps you are beginning your new life as a college student, entering the workforce, or starting a family of your own.

In all these cases, you are following in the steps of someone. A former colleague. Your parents. Friends. But for you, it's your own personal journey. You've never gone down this road before.

Or maybe you are in your twilight years and want to check a few items off the bucket list. You don't have to be ordinary. You can set the standard and blaze a trail that is unique and inspirational.

PLAYER INTRODUCTIONS

Chances are you will never be in a position to win a national title like Tubby, but you can still be a trailblazer.

You may not receive fanfare or appear in television interviews, but that's okay. As long as you achieve personal fulfillment, that is all that matters.

The first key is to not worry about what others think. This doesn't mean you ignore advice, but do not let the opinions and judgments of others stop you in your quest for excellence.

When you get dunked on, and you will, hustle back to the other end of the court and get ready for the next play. Put the past behind you and look ahead for positive results.

Never be afraid to use your voice to speak up. Make an impact on the people in your life. This might mean becoming involved in your community or finding a unique way to be heard. Instead of complaining, step up and take action toward positive change.

Muster up the courage to start your journey as soon as possible. Take a risk and move forward. There might be challenges along the way but be committed to yourself and plow ahead.

If there are people on your team who hog the ball and won't let you participate, find another squad that will include you as part of the team. Rid yourself of negative people. This might be difficult to do, but it will allow you to put yourself on a championship team that appreciates your efforts.

Always appreciate milestones and moments throughout your trip. Make friends with people you encounter every day. Smile at the person who gives you coffee and take time to be friendly with strangers.

You don't have to play the perfect game but try your best to get good results. Forget about trying to be perfect and focus on what you can bring to the court.

Own up to your mistakes and learn from them. Never make excuses or put yourself down for trying to do something new.

If you fail, so what? Try. Set the standard and keep going. Just like Tubby Smith.

And finally, believe in who you are and what you can do. You will never win a game unless you first show up at the arena. Lace up your shoes and get on the court. You have something to offer.

Blaze the trail.

Go Big Blue.

What can you do to be a trailblazer? It might be simple things you never thought about before.

_____

_____

_____

_____

_____

_____

WEEK 33 | THE END OF THE BEGINNING

SATURDAY, MARCH 18, 1972, MARKED the end of the beginning of the Kentucky Basketball program. That was the day
that UK's legendary coach Adolph Rupp coached his final game
for the Wildcats. Oh, there was basketball in Lexington prior
to Rupp's arrival, but it was the Baron of the Bluegrass himself
who planted Kentucky at the pinnacle of the college basketball
mountain.

The setting that day was the NCAA Mideast regional finals
held in front of 13,458 fans at the University of Dayton Arena
in Dayton, Ohio. History will show that tenth-ranked Florida
State, under Coach Hugh Durham, defeated eighteenth-ranked
Kentucky 73–54 to end Rupp's magnificent run. For Kentucky
fans, the loss was disheartening—but it was the significance of
the moment that would clearly resonate within their hearts and
minds for decades to come.

Afterward, Rupp officially "retired," but the reality was that
he left UK kicking and screaming, trying tirelessly to buck the
state-mandated retirement age of seventy in effect at that time
for university employees.

For the record, Jim Andrews led Kentucky against the Seminoles that day with 17 points and 11 rebounds. Tom Parker and

Ronnie Lyons chipped in with 10 points apiece. Larry Stamper, Stan Key, Bob McCowan, and Rick Drewitz rounded out the box score—and thus became important footnotes in Kentucky Basketball days of yore.

It all began with the Baron.

Adolph Rupp was born in Halstead, Kansas, in 1901. He attended the University of Kansas, and as a reserve on the Jayhawk basketball team, he played for legendary Kansas coach Phog Allen, who was himself a disciple of James Naismith—the inventor of the game. Armed with that impressive pedigree, Rupp subsequently secured a couple of high school coaching jobs before landing a spot in the coveted college ranks at the University of Kentucky.

Rupp, known as the "Man in the Brown Suit" (he once lost wearing a blue suit and swore never to wear one again), would go on to build a dynasty in Lexington over the next forty-one years. From 1931 through 1972, he won 876 games—and remained the winningest coach in all of college basketball until North Carolina's Dean Smith passed him in 1997. During his reign, UK won four NCAA titles (1948, 1949, 1951, 1958), one Olympic gold medal (1948), one NIT championship when it still meant something (1946), and twenty-seven Southeastern Conference titles and had six number-one final poll rankings.

Rupp coached many great players during his tenure at Kentucky. Names like Ralph Beard, Alex Groza, Cliff Hagan, Frank Ramsey, Johnny Cox, Vernon Hatton, Cotton Nash, Pat Riley, and Dan Issel still roll off the tongue like a smooth shot of Kentucky bourbon. All in all, twenty-six of his players were voted to the All-American team forty-four different times.

Rupp, a four-time National Coach of the Year and a seven-time SEC Coach of the Year, was inducted into the Naismith Hall of Fame in 1969. Interestingly, Rupp died on December 10, 1977—the night Kentucky defeated Kansas 73–66 on Adolph Rupp Night at his Jayhawk alma mater.

Even with all that success, the one burning question that has divided the Kentucky fan base recently is whether Adolph Rupp was a racist. Pundits from both sides of the aisle have put forth compelling arguments to support their positions. The truth is that regardless of the evidence presented, we'll never know what was in Rupp's heart at the time.

What we do know is that without Adolph Rupp, there would be no beginning to the great program that exists today. Without a doubt, he remains the most important figure in Kentucky Basketball's glorious history. That's how he should be remembered.

END OF THE SEASON

Everyone questions what legacy they will leave. Some begin the planning stages early in life, while some don't have any clue until their later years. And for some, they might be remembered for something they would never have intended.

Hopefully, you will go out held in high regard by most, but you will need to accept the fact that you will never please everyone.

For the most part, the way you are remembered is up to you. You can have visions and hopes of what will happen in the end, but in all honesty, you will not be around to know what impact you truly had.

However, you can set the stage for the best outcome possible.

TOURNAMENT RUN

No one wants to live with regrets.

When it's your time to step away from the limelight, you don't want to be haunted by past mistakes. Negative thoughts and bad memories can affect your legacy and your mental well-being.

Possess the courage to live your life true to yourself and to your family.

You don't want to look back later and wish you had demonstrated the guts to do the right thing at the right time.

Make sure your priorities are in check.

On your retirement day, will you reflect on all the things you were never able to accomplish? Will you spend your senior years thinking about missed opportunities? Or will you leave your career with the satisfaction that you gave it your all and did your best?

Hopefully, you will be able to cherish the memories of taking the time to attend your children's school and sports functions and maintain a work-life balance. These fond recollections will be worth more than the gold watch you receive at your farewell party.

Being honored as a loyal worker is fine, but it's not worth it if you sacrificed your relationships with friends and family in order to receive those accolades.

Also, don't be afraid to express your feelings to the people you love. Waiting to do this could be a devastating regret. Maybe you did not tell your mother or father how much they meant to you when they were still living, and now it's too late. Be sure to let your spouse, children, and friends know while they are still with you.

If you are estranged from loved ones, make the effort to reconcile. Even if you are unsuccessful, at least you will have the peace of knowing that you gave it your best effort.

Don't let any more time slip away. Your legacy and the enjoyment of your retirement years are at stake. You cannot control what some people might think of you, but you can let them know where you stand. Even if they don't agree, they will respect your position.

Allow yourself to be happy. Life is too short, and you are not guaranteed an overtime period.

Do it for Big Blue Nation!

How will you prevent regrets from taking control of your life?

WEEK 34 | MR. WILDCAT

ONE THING KENTUCKY FANS MAY have noticed recently is that there's a wall going up between UK greats of the past and present. Perhaps *wall* is too strong of a word. Let's call it a bit of a "disconnect" instead. Players who played in previous eras don't quite feel the love from the current regime anymore. It's natural for this type of tension to simmer. After all, you can't expect a coach to develop relationships with former players he didn't coach that are as strong as relationships he developed with his own charges.

As much as John Calipari has attempted to incorporate past UK greats as part of "La Familia," things just haven't been the same since the passing of Bill Keightley.

Keightley, known affectionately within BBN as "Mr. Wildcat," served as the equipment manager for the UK basketball team for forty-eight years. But his role involved much more than just gathering socks and jocks. He was a mentor for players who sought advice and a sounding board for those who just wanted to vent. Always quick with a word of encouragement or a smile, he was the perfect father figure, confidant, and liaison between the UK players and the six coaches (Adolph Rupp, Joe B. Hall, Eddie Sutton, Rick Pitino, Tubby Smith, and Billy Gillispie) under which he served.

Already grandfatherly in appearance, Keightley's disdain for the University of Louisville further endeared him to all of the BBN. He'd be like a kid on Christmas morning looking forward to those annual rivalry games between the Cats and the Cards. The tension coursing through his body—sitting on the bench suffering through the game action—made everyone hyperventilate. His love for the Wildcats was deep, passionate, and as genuine as could be.

Born on December 17, 1926, in Lawrenceburg, Kentucky, Keightley served as a marine in World War II and was working as a postal carrier when a coworker asked him to help out as an assistant equipment manager for the UK basketball team. Little did he know, as fate would have it, that he would become the official man in charge of the entire UK locker room a mere decade later.

On March 31, 2008, Keightley fell while traveling on his annual trip to watch his beloved Cincinnati Reds on Baseball's Opening Day at Great American Ballpark. He was taken to a hospital and died later that day due to internal bleeding caused by a previously undiagnosed cancerous tumor on his spine.

When Bill Keightley died, he took a major part of the UK program with him. He was that one tangible connection between Wildcat eras. If he were still alive today, he'd be the glue cementing Sam Bowie with Karl-Anthony Towns, that necessary catalyst for the smooth transition between Kyle Macy and John Wall. It didn't matter how long ago or how recently you wore the jersey, former players returning for visits felt as welcome as they did on senior night. Greeted by that familiar smile and that welcoming "hey, buddy," players felt as if they had never left the court.

Sadly, for Kentucky fans and players alike, it's just not like it used to be without Mr. Wildcat around.

"He's the spirit of the program," said Jim Host—founder of Host Communications, the sports marketing and production empire bearing his name—when he heard that Keightley had died. "I just can't believe he won't be sitting there on that bench. Of all people, he was symbolic of the program."

Fans, players, coaches, officials, and administrators—everybody dearly misses Mr. Wildcat.

POSTGAME

You don't have to be at the top of the hierarchy in your organization to be an essential part of the team. In fact, it's often the people behind the scenes who serve as the glue that holds the team together.

Take pride in supporting your team and make it a priority to inspire your colleagues to exhibit their creativity and innovation. Never forget those who laid the groundwork to make your team the success it is today. Your passion for life will inspire and encourage others, and you should always cheer your coworkers on to victory.

What you do off the court often stands out more than what you do when the ball is tipped in the air.

TURN OFF THE LIGHTS

There are many things you can do to be considered your own version of "Mr. Wildcat":

Smile at people.
Hold the door open for someone coming into a restaurant behind you.
Pay for the coffee for the person behind you in the drive-through.
Take an evening snack to the nurses at your local hospice facility.

Send get-well cards to people you know who are elderly and
   shut in.
Volunteer your time with a local charity.
Become involved in your community.
Coach your kid's Little League team.
Pitch in to help during a neighborhood cleanup day.
Do yard work for a widow in your community.
These are just some suggestions, but you get the idea.

Bill Keightley was remembered for his passion and love for
Kentucky Basketball. You can be remembered for the passion
and love shown to your family and friends.

When you are eager and excited about what you do, it can be
contagious for those around you. Don't just put in your eight
hours on the job and go home. Work to make a positive difference and find ways to enrich the lives of others.

Be passionate about life. Be the glue that holds your team together.

Big Blue Nation!

How can you become more passionate?

_____
_____
_____
_____
_____
_____
_____
_____

WEEK 35 | IT'S BUSINESS

IN HIS BOOK *CUT TO THE CHASE*, Alan Cutler of LEX18 tells about the first time he interviewed Jamal Mashburn. The "Monster Mash" was a newly minted UK freshman who talked enthusiastically about playing in the NBA. That wasn't unusual for new UK recruits. What was unusual was Mashburn making an unsolicited pitch about becoming a future successful businessman.

If serving as a television analyst for ESPN; being a stakeholder in over a hundred franchises (including Outback Steakhouse, Papa John's Pizza, and Dunkin' Donuts); becoming a partner in some major car dealerships (Toyota and Lexus); having ownership interest in real estate, hotels, and the thoroughbred horse racing industry; and sitting on the advisory board of well-respected banks qualifies as business success, then the UK All-American who always wanted to carry a briefcase to work is a very happy man. Throw in an eleven-year NBA career averaging 19.1 points per game on top of all those business ventures, and you could make an argument that Mashburn is one of the most successful Wildcat players ever.

If not the most successful Wildcat, then Jamal Mashburn certainly qualifies as perhaps the most important Kentucky recruit ever. Coming out of Cardinal Hayes High School in the Bronx, the 6'8" 240-pound Parade All-American was Mr. Basketball in the state of New York in 1990. Kentucky fans will remember that time period well. The vaunted UK program was still on probation—recovering from the shame and humiliation of the Emery package and ACT cheating scandal. Rick Pitino had been hired to lead the Wildcats back into the Promised Land—and landing a recruit of Mashburn's stature was paramount to the mission at hand.

Mashburn did not disappoint. In his freshman year, he averaged nearly 13 points a game and led Kentucky to an amazing 22–6 record. That Kentucky team finished out the regular season by beating Auburn in a memorable 114–93 rout, establishing themselves unequivocally as the best in the league.

The league standings, however, were marked with an asterisk because Kentucky was technically ineligible for the SEC title due to their probationary status. But as Richie Farmer famously said—amid the fan celebration and parade held in their honor—as far as the official standings were concerned, they could "kiss my asterisk."

Against the Tigers, Mashburn led the team with 21 points before 24,310 fans—the then-largest crowd in Rupp Arena history. The very next year, as a sophomore, he would carry the Wildcats to an NCAA tournament regional final. In his junior season, Mashburn would take Kentucky one step further, all the way to the Final Four—their first appearance in nearly a decade . . . and just a scant two years removed from being left for dead.

In 1993, after being selected as a consensus All-American and First Team All-SEC and being voted the SEC Player of the Year, Mashburn declared early for the NBA draft. He was selected number four overall in the first round by the Dallas Mavericks.

Although Mashburn doesn't make it back to Lexington as often as fans would like, he remains forever civic-minded toward the university community. Even before he signed his first professional basketball contract, he donated $500,000 to establish a scholarship fund at his alma mater.

Jamal Mashburn deciding to play basketball at the University of Kentucky remains one of the most significant milestones in the program's history. Although fans primarily remember him for being a savior on the court, his achievements in the business world are even more laudatory.

THE ALL-AMERICAN RECRUIT

Perhaps you have faced a similar situation to that of UK Basketball. You are on "probation" and trying to establish a positive image for yourself. You may be rebounding from legal issues, or someone you love may have lost trust in you. It's time for a fresh start. Or a do-over.

A job loss or a personal breakup might have you on the sidelines. Or maybe you are discouraged by an illness or the loss of a friend.

Have circumstances outside of your control caused you to question your identity?

Who are you?

CREATE YOUR OWN HYPE

You always have time to start over. There are always opportunities to make a wrong right. It might take some time, but the investment will be worth it in the end. Land that prized recruit.

Consider furthering your education, and sacrifice time spent with hobbies and entertainment to learn something new.

Maybe you need a change of scenery or a fresh outlook on life.

But this doesn't always mean physically picking everything up and moving.

It can often be the little things.

Walk through a park and clean up the trash. Beautify an area in your community that has grown over. Recognize the treasure it can be to other families in your region.

Rake leaves or cut the grass for a widow who lives nearby, or volunteer to pick up her medicine and groceries.

Spend time at a homeless shelter or serve food at a soup kitchen. If you have children, volunteer and become involved in their activities. Coach your kid's team, or work in the concession stand.

You have potential and promise. Don't let the circumstances of the past direct your future.

You might have a debt to pay, but work toward a goal, and be determined to make it to the big leagues and fulfill your dreams, even if they are different from what people expect from you. Jamal Mashburn's dreams went far beyond the basketball court, and he used his experience at UK and in the NBA to set himself up for success in the business world. But he also remembered to stop along the way to help take care of others.

You can also succeed with the right attitude and drive. Mend the wrongs of the past, work toward a rewarding future, and show compassion for others along the way.

Go Big Blue!

What potential do you have?

How can you reach your goals?

_____

_____

_____

_____

_____

_____

WEEK 36 | THE REAL FABULOUS FIVE

BEFORE THERE WAS CHRIS WEBBER, Jalen Rose, Juwan Howard, Jimmy King, and Ray Jackson—the heralded "Fab Five" from the 1991 University of Michigan recruiting class—there was the real "Fabulous Five" from the University of Kentucky.

That 1948 Wildcat squad accomplished more than any other college team in the history of the sport. Not only did they win the NCAA championship that year, but they went on to win an Olympic gold medal. Why they didn't get more credit for what they achieved leaves many a longtime UK basketball fan completely bumfuzzled.

On March 23, 1948, in front of 16,174 fans at the Old Madison Square Garden in New York City, Kentucky's Fabulous Five of Wallace "Wah Wah" Jones, Alex Groza, Cliff Barker, Ralph Beard, and Kenny Rollins defeated Baylor 58–42 to win the school's first national title.

The Wildcats, behind the team-leading 14-point effort from Groza, jumped out to an early 17-point lead and never looked back. The five starters played the entire first thirty-three and a half minutes of the ballgame without taking a breather as they completely dominated the outclassed and outsized Bears from Waco. As the champions were crowned, the 6'7" Groza was voted the most outstanding player of the tournament.

Kentucky then entered the Olympic qualifying tournament, defeating none other than the Louisville Cardinals 91–57 in the first round. They would eventually lose in the finals to the AAU Phillips 66ers. But despite the loss, all five of the Fabulous Five were named to the US Olympic team roster.

Throughout the Olympic competition, the Fabulous Five spent much of their time on the court together, displaying the teamwork and cohesiveness necessary in going for the gold. Blowout victories over Switzerland, Czechoslovakia, Egypt, Peru, Uruguay, and Mexico—and a 59–57 squeaker over Argentina—set up the gold medal showdown against France.

On August 13, 1948, in Harringay Arena in London, before an estimated crowd of six thousand—one of the largest to ever witness a basketball contest in Britain—the United States easily defeated France 65–21. Groza once again led all scorers with 11 points.

The next year, the dominance continued. On March 26, 1949, at the Edmondson Pavilion in Seattle, Washington, the Fabulous Five (minus Rollins, who had graduated) led number-one-ranked Kentucky to a 46–36 victory over number-two-ranked Oklahoma A&M for the school's second title trophy. Groza was top scorer again with a 25-point effort in the championship game.

Kentucky fans love happy endings. Unfortunately, the story of the real Fabulous Five doesn't fit the bill. Groza and Beard were later implicated in a point-shaving scandal, placed on indefinite probation, and banned from playing in the NBA. Perhaps that's the real reason the Fabulous Five haven't gotten the love that they should have. As far as basketball achievements are concerned, it's as if their legacy has been redacted.

Beard admits he took money—but claims he never for one second influenced the score of a basketball game. The truth is that he made a horrible mistake and paid dearly for it with his basketball career.

That shouldn't discredit what he and the real Fabulous Five accomplished in their time at UK. My goodness—two consecutive NCAA championships and an Olympic gold medal would become nearly impossible feats to follow.

COME OFF THE SCREEN

Maybe you and your team are like the Fabulous Five. Over the years, you have received accolades for accomplishments and headlines from family, friends, and coworkers. Perhaps your employer even recognized your hard work with bonuses or extra days off.

Hopefully, your hard work is rewarded. But oftentimes, it's not. Since others forget easily, many of us like to display plaques, certificates, and photos in our offices to remind others of our accomplishments.

But symbols of recognition are often not necessary when you publicly make a mistake. Everyone remembers and associates you with these errors. And sometimes they follow you and paint the wrong picture. Has this happened to you?

GO TO THE BUCKET

Everyone goofs up. The magnitude of your blunder doesn't seem to matter. If you have paid your debt to society in some way, via personal restitution, a public apology, or through legal means, you can start over.

Your biggest obstacle might be to forgive yourself.

If you are like me, you are harder on yourself than anyone. This is because you didn't live up to your own standards and expectations.

If you have made a mistake, it's okay to be disappointed in yourself—but don't let that last, take you into depression, and limit your ability to come back.

The UK Basketball team had some losses, but they rebounded and kept winning.

Be disappointed in yourself for a night, but then develop and implement a game plan to get back on the winning track.

Learn the hard lessons from your mistakes and be determined to raise another championship banner. You can do it. Don't let "yourself" get in the way.

Watch the game film and see where you messed up.

However, don't obsess on your missed assignment. Instead, use it as motivation to win the gold in the end.

Make a checklist of goals you want to accomplish and allow enough time to achieve them. You might have to climb your way back up the ladder and get a taste of your own medicine. Most of the time, the flavor is bitter on the way down, but it makes you better in the long run.

Go Cats!

How can you learn from your mistakes?

What are your plans to return to your winning ways?

_____

_____

_____

_____

_____

_____

_____

_____

_____

_____

_____

_____

WEEK 37 | BEFORE "BO KNOWS"

LONGTIME SPORTS FANS ARE FAMILIAR with Bo Jackson, the multisport star who played both baseball for the Kansas City Royals and football for the Los Angeles Raiders. In 1989, Nike launched a game-changing series of commercials depicting Jackson playing every sport imaginable as part of the ad campaign for their new cross-trainer sneakers. Everyone remembers the tagline "Bo Knows"—a phrase that magically granted Jackson superstar powers in every sport he tried.

Before there was "Bo Knows," there was Charles "Cotton" Nash.

Nash was a 6'5" gifted athlete with a nickname to match. As a youngster, his blond hair was nearly white. A sportswriter fawning over his Little League prowess dubbed him "Cotton"— and the moniker stuck.

Nash played for the Wildcats from 1961 through 1964—a time considered by Kentucky fans to be a lull between eras. Gone were the glory days of the "Fiddlin' Five," while "Rupp's Runts" hadn't quite come on the scene. During his junior season, Nash almost singlehandedly dragged his team to nineteen wins while nursing a nagging foot injury. Because the wins were rather pedestrian, Nash never received the glowing accolades he deserved.

On December 31, 1963, during Nash's senior season, Kentucky played Duke in the Sugar Bowl Championships in New Orleans. It was a huge game for both teams. Duke featured All-American scorer Jeff Mullins, a 6'4" former Mr. Basketball from Lafayette High School in Lexington.

The Wildcats, who had just clawed their way back to a number-one ranking, fell behind the ninth-ranked Blue Devils early. Down by 10 at the half and still trailing 66–58 with less than eleven minutes to go in the game, the Cats mounted a rally against their much taller opponents.

With just three seconds left and the score tied at 79, Kentucky's Randy Embry whipped a pass over to Terry Mobley, who banked in a thirteen-foot jumper for the dramatic 81–79 UK victory. Mobley got the glory for his last-second heroics, but as usual, it was Nash who led the team with 30 points.

During his time at Kentucky, Nash was a three-time All-SEC First Team selection and a three-time consensus All-American. His 22.7 point-per-game average is second only to Dan Issel, and he ranks ninth on the all-time career points leaderboard. But it was really for his time after UK that Nash earned his legendary "Bo Knows" status.

Nash was drafted number twelve overall in the second round of the 1964 NBA draft by the Los Angeles Lakers. Prior to reporting to their training camp, Nash played a hundred or so games of minor league baseball for the California Angels. He then returned to the Lakers to start his professional basketball career. After a full season of basketball, he was right back to the grind of baseball spring training.

Nash made his Major League debut with the Chicago White Sox on September 1, 1967. During that stint, the ABA started up their brand-new league. Playing professional basketball in Louisville was too good of an opportunity to pass up, so Nash signed on to play for the Kentucky Colonels during their inaugural

1967–1968 season. He also continued his Major League career, making his last big-league appearance for the Minnesota Twins on October 1, 1970.

It's rare nowadays to have multisport stars. The game is way too specialized and the training far too focused. Back in the late '80s, Bo knew how do to it. And as UK fans remember, "Cotton" Nash knew how to do it too . . . a full two decades earlier.

PREGAME PRESS CONFERENCE

If you want to be a contender, no matter what you set your sights on doing, you must master the ability to do one thing: learn.

You must grow as a person and develop the skill to understand and adapt.

It makes sense and is worth the investment to make an effort to absorb new surroundings.

Perhaps you want to go back to school and obtain that degree you've dreamed about for years. Or maybe you have a desire to step out of your comfort zone and take a chance on owning your own business.

Discover the talents that make you unique. Never let anyone tell you that you are ordinary.

"Cotton" Nash certainly was not ordinary. He took advantage of opportunities and used his abilities to the max.

SHOWTIME

Life comes down to being coachable.

Making the most of your ability means being honest with yourself and leaving your ego in the locker room.

Take action and start learning a new skill. This means practice. Nash was a natural athlete, but he still had to practice his shooting and ball-handling skills every day.

Apply what you have been taught to improve your skills.

Adopt a mindset of continuous improvement. If you don't search for avenues to become better, you will be stuck in the same place as others pass you by on the way to success.

Progress is the key. Move forward and view each challenge as a great opportunity to learn.

It's okay to make a mistake. Just try to avoid making the same one twice.

In order to learn, you must have a cooperative environment. Find inspiration or encouragement in devotional books or quotes. Set aside a special time to find inner strength.

Pay attention to your surroundings and to roadblocks that can hold you back.

Michael Jordan, one of the greatest players ever to play basketball, once said his greatest skill was not dunking a ball, dribbling, or defense. He said it was being teachable and willing to learn.

You might be a fantastic employee, parent, or spouse, but you can always do better. Strive every day to look for ways to improve yourself to benefit those around you. They deserve the best you that you can be.

Make the most of your abilities. Explore different opportunities.

Go Big Blue!

What are three things you can do to learn new things? Are you coachable?

_____

_____

_____

_____

_____

WEEK 38 | THE "UNTOUCHABLES"

THE 1995–1996 UNIVERSITY OF KENTUCKY Wildcat Basketball team was the greatest UK team ever assembled. There's a reason they've been dubbed the "Untouchables." They only lost two games the entire season, and most of their victories were of the blowout variety.

That team, consisting of five future first-round NBA draft picks (Tony Delk, Antoine Walker, Walter McCarty, Derek Anderson, and Ron Mercer), took no prisoners on their scorched-earth march to a championship. Along the way, they averaged 91.4 points per contest, pummeled eleven different opponents by 30 points or more, scored 86 points in one half versus LSU, and hung 120 points on the hapless Vanderbilt Commodores.

When tournament time came rolling around, they were just as ruthless. A 110–72 thrashing of San Jose State, an 84–60 thumping of Virginia Tech, a 101–70 romp over Utah, and an 83–63 dismantling of Tim Duncan and the Wake Forest Demon Deacons sent the team barreling into the Final Four with a full head of steam.

On March 30, 1996—Semifinal Saturday at Continental Arena in East Rutherford, New Jersey—the number-two-ranked "Untouchables" were matched up against John Calipari's number-one-ranked UMass Minutemen, a worthy opponent that had previously defeated Kentucky 92–82 in the second game of the season. The Cats came out bent on revenge, capitalizing on several UMass turnovers for an 11–2 run that staked them to a 36–28 halftime lead.

In the second half, Kentucky built the lead up to 15, but UMass—behind Marcus Camby's game-high 25 points—would slowly fight back. The Minutemen were still down 10 with 2:35 to go when they mounted one final furious rally. With just 1:02 left on the clock, Edgar Padilla drilled a three-pointer, and suddenly the score was 73–70. But Kentucky didn't flinch; they played smart, held on by hitting their last 8 free throws, and escaped with an 81–74 heart-pounding win.

Two nights later, it was Kentucky versus Syracuse for all the marbles. This was Tony Delk's night to shine. The senior guard from Brownsville, Tennessee, shot a record 7 of 12 from behind the arc to lead the Wildcats with 24 points. With 11:12 to play in the game, Delk somehow got a three-pointer to fall while being fouled and tumbling to the floor in front of the Kentucky bench. His follow-up foul shot gave the Cats a 59–46 lead they would not relinquish.

Other than Delk, the Wildcats struggled mightily all night against the Orangemen's patented 2-3 zone, hitting only 38 percent of their shots from the field. Syracuse, behind John Wallace's 29-point effort, kept pounding away. With less than five minutes to play, Kentucky found themselves clinging to a precarious 64–62 lead.

An offensive rebound by McCarty, a twenty-two-foot jumper by Anderson, and a six-foot jumper in the lane by Mark Pope gave the Cats some breathing room. With two minutes on the clock, however, Jim Boeheim's team made one final push. Todd Burgan's three-point bomb cut the lead back down to 5. But

Wallace fouled out at the 1:06 mark, and Kentucky held on for the 76–67 win.

It was Kentucky's sixth national title, and the first championship trophy in eighteen years—secured by a team that was indeed "Untouchable."

WARM UP

Your day is approaching, and you are excited to make your mark on the world, or at least on your community.

You've completed college or trade school, or you have made other preparations to enter the workforce.

Or maybe you are trying to chase a dream and begin a new adventure.

You have, in your opinion, assembled a team that cannot lose. You have the confidence needed to pull out the big victory. It can be anything in life—a new career, a new relationship, or a big rebound from a setback life dunked on you.

No matter the case, you must be ready for the championship game.

Life can play out on the most glamourous stage, or it can be done solo with no one watching you play.

Getting your life together doesn't have to be complicated.

SCORCH THE NETS

The first thing a good coach or player does is to review their strengths and weaknesses with an honest approach.

If you struggle to identify your own strengths and weaknesses, ask your friends or family for their input, and write it down. You don't have to agree, but you also should not be in denial. Listen and take notes.

This will lead you to a self-examination, and that should lead to a game plan.

The best coaches in the world do this to prepare for the big game. They never go into a contest without a strategy to win.

Outcomes don't just happen. You need to work actively toward reaching a goal and making needed changes.

Be willing to learn and adapt on the fly. If you have a goal in mind, the best way to motivate and inspire yourself is to incorporate positive change. Always be on the lookout for new ways to learn from people you admire. Don't try to imitate or try to be like them but try to adopt a similar approach to life.

While you shouldn't rush the development of your plan, overthinking it can lead to procrastination and second-guessing. Put a good sound plan together and get busy. The longer you toss the details around in your mind, the more doubt will creep in.

It's also a good idea to track your progress and keep a journal to write down what worked and what needs to be changed. Document all the things you do well and every task completed, and track your progress going forward so you'll know if you're on target.

Put it all together with a positive attitude and mindset.

Delete all negative self-talk from your vocabulary. Think only positive thoughts and speak only positive words from now on. If you make mistakes, own up to them and move forward. You won't grow unless you accept them and make things right.

Examine criticism, but don't let it stop you. Some of it may be constructive and worthy of evaluation, but some may just be interference that you can't let distract you from your goal.

Think like a leader and surround yourself with dependable people who have your best interests in mind and can sort out the good advice from the attempts to sabotage your success.

The Kentucky Wildcats put together the "Untouchables," who had one unified goal—to work together as a team to win it all.

You can do the same. Be determined, resolute, and "untouchable" in your approach to success.

Go Big Blue!

How can you put your plan together?

_____

_____

_____

_____

_____

_____

_____

_____

_____

_____

_____

_____

_____

_____

_____

_____

_____

_____

_____

_____

_____

_____

_____

WEEK 39 | THE BEST THINGS IN LIFE ARE THREES

"YOU DON'T HAVE TO MAKE them all. You just can't miss them all."

That was Kentucky coach John Calipari on March 15, 2018, on the podium in Boise, Idaho, just minutes after his team defeated Davidson 78–73 in their opening-round game of the NCAA tournament. Calipari was referencing the three-point shot, lamenting the fact that Kentucky's streak—extending all the way back to 1988—of 1,047 consecutive games of making at least one three-pointer was dead on arrival that night. Although they savored the victory, there was a bittersweet sense among all of BBN of having to finally say goodbye to a lifelong friend.

Kentucky fans have always been fascinated with the three-point shot. That's certainly understandable because there's been a slew of them throughout the course of their team's glorious history.

Aaron Harrison's game winners during that 2015 tournament run have to be at the top of everybody's list. Scott Padgett's "three-pointer heard around the world" versus Duke, Tony Delk's bomb while being fouled and falling out of bounds against Syracuse, and Walter McCarty's Mardi Gras Miracle against LSU would undoubtedly be next in line. How about

Tayshaun Prince and his 5 consecutive threes to begin the game versus North Carolina?

Had Kentucky won these contests, Patrick Sparks's rim rattler against Michigan State or Anthony Epps's double-clutch swish versus Arizona would also be in the running. But if you're talking about the pure emotion of memorable trifectas made under big-game situations, you'd be hard-pressed to find one that's more soul-stirring than this.

It happened on Sunday, March 27, 2011, at the Prudential Center in Newark, New Jersey. Eleventh-ranked Kentucky was facing off against the seventh-ranked North Carolina Tar Heels for a chance to advance to the Final Four in Houston. The Cats were coming off a monumental upset of number-one-ranked Ohio State just two days earlier. Brandon Knight—arguably one of the most underrated Kentucky one-and-dones of all time—drilled a fifteen-foot jumper with 5.4 seconds left (and Aaron Craft's hand in his face) to secure the 62–60 win. Knight had already worn the hero's cape earlier in the tournament—hitting a last-second game-winning driving layup against Princeton and saving Kentucky from punching an early ticket back home to Lexington.

As expected, the tilt with the Tar Heels was a made-for-television thriller. North Carolina, with future NBA stars Harrison Barnes, Tyler Zeller, and John Henson, fell behind early. Kentucky, behind Knight's game-high 22 points, quickly took control and pulled out to a 38–30 halftime lead.

The Wildcats stretched the lead to 11 in the second half, when Carolina finally made its run. With a minute to go, Carolina had the ball trailing by only one when DeAndre Liggins came up with a huge block on the defensive end of the court. Then, on Kentucky's subsequent possession with thirty-seven seconds to go, Liggins drilled the dramatic three-point dagger from the corner that essentially secured the victory. Kentucky would go on to win 76–69 on the way to their first Final Four appearance in thirteen years. The pure emotion of the win was captured perfectly in the famous image of Calipari embracing Liggins as he strutted triumphantly off the court.

In one of the greatest quotes in Kentucky Basketball history, Antoine Walker was asked why he shot so many threes: "Because there are no fours," he famously quipped.

Kentucky Basketball fans love their threes . . . and the stories about the heroes who made them.

THE REBOUND

Everyone wants their life to matter. To count. No one wants to be forgotten. No one wants to be remembered for the wrong reasons.

But life is not a Final Four championship game every day. While there are many memories you can celebrate, many others are peppered with struggles and defeats.

This is true. You might lose more than you win. But that should never deter you from taking some three-point shots and trying to get positive results.

You will experience frustrations in relationships, on the job, and perhaps even with your health. Life does not grant you a win with a three-pointer at the buzzer every day.

TAKE THE SHOTS

You are on this court of life for four short quarters. Make the most of your opportunities to score.

Your career is important, but it's not what defines you, or at least it should not be.

Many people put wealth and status at the top of the list of indicators that define success.

A three-point shot can have an enormous impact on a game. It can change the momentum and ultimately the outcome of a contest.

You can have the same impact in life by going the extra mile.

One way to do this is to make life about others and not focus solely on yourself. You are not the center of the universe, but you might be the center of your family. Make them your top priority, and work to have a positive impact on them.

Another way of doing extra is to give more and receive less. It's okay to reward yourself with new purchases sometimes, but also think of ways you can spread the wealth. Instead of buying that boat, consider making a large donation to a charity or church. If you are not in a position to give financially, you can give something more valuable—your time.

Instead of seeking new ways to satisfy yourself, look to enhance the lives of those in your family or community.

Wake up with an attitude of service, and ask yourself, "How can I serve my loved ones today?"

What can you do to go the extra mile to make someone's day? Maybe send a card or a special gift. Make phone calls to check up on elderly friends or just to let them know you are thinking of them. They will appreciate the concern, and it might make them smile and feel loved.

Go Big Blue!

How can you go the extra mile for someone?

_____

_____

_____

_____

POSTSEASON
SPRINT

WEEK 40 | LOOK MOM, WE MADE IT!

"ALL THAT I AM, OR hope to be, I owe to my angel mother."

The above quote was attributed to Abraham Lincoln, but it could very well have come directly from Bam Adebayo. The current rising superstar for the Miami Heat was raised by his single mom in a single-wide trailer home in eastern North Carolina. While working at her $12,000-a-year job as a cashier in a butcher shop, Adebayo's mom, Marilyn Blount, made sure Bam had every chance to succeed in basketball and in life. Seeing how his mom sacrificed everything for him, Bam decided at a ripe young age to make a life-changing promise to himself.

"My whole devotion became to get my mom out of that trailer," he told Zach Lowe of *Sports Illustrated* in a 2020 feature article.

Bam's dedication and singular focus landed him a scholarship at the University of Kentucky. During his one-and-done season in 2016–2017, the 6'8" 230-pound center was a scoring and rebounding machine. While at UK, he set the Calipari-era record for all-time double-doubles with eight. And they weren't just "barely" double-doubles against no-name competition either. Bam put up 22 points and 15 rebounds against both Missouri and Florida in consecutive games down the conference stretch.

Kentucky fans remember Bam as being an extremely hard-working, unselfish teammate. He did what his coaches told him to do, and he kept his nose squeaky clean off the court. Though he felt more than capable of handling the ball and shooting threes from the perimeter, Calipari needed him to play defense and to be a presence down low—so Bam complied. Just as importantly, he attended class regularly, smiled a lot, and became popular with teammates and fans alike.

Bam saved his best performances for the first two rounds of the NCAA tournament. On March 17, 2017, in number-five-ranked Kentucky's 79–70 win over Northern Kentucky, Bam pulled down an eye-popping 18 boards to go along with his 15 points. He followed that up with a 13-point, 10-rebound effort two nights later to will Kentucky to a hard-fought 65–62 grinder over nineteenth-ranked Wichita State.

At the conclusion of the season—after the Cats fell one game shy of another Final Four—Bam elected to follow his dreams by putting his name into the upcoming NBA draft.

On June 22, 2017, at the Barclays Center in Brooklyn, New York, Edrice "Bam" Adebayo fulfilled that solemn promise he made back in his youth. Drafted number fourteen overall in the first round by Miami, Adebayo became an instant millionaire. Repaying his mom for her unconditional love would no longer be a pipedream. Life in the trailer was over forever.

Coach John Calipari talks frequently of ending generational poverty. And for many like Bam, the path to riches passes directly through Lexington. Forty-one NBA draft picks, thirty-one first-rounders, twenty-one lottery selections, and three number-one picks in Coach Cal's first eleven years at UK amounts to millions and millions of contract dollars. As you read this, the numbers continue to rise.

Calipari also talks frequently about finding your "why"—your motivation for doing what you do.

For Bam Adebayo, his "why" was always clear—to take care of his mom and repay the woman who always took care of him.

TWO-A-DAY SESSIONS

Parents. If you have them, you are blessed.

Hopefully, you had both a mother and father who cared and sacrificed for you. Or maybe it was your grandparents. Sadly, this is not always the story.

Not everyone enjoys a healthy parental relationship. Perhaps there were circumstances beyond your control that led to a distant or even nonexistent relationship with your parents. You might be thinking, "You don't know what I went through." This is understandable, but it might also be an opportunity for you to offer forgiveness even if they don't ask for it. This may not solve everything, but it will certainly start you down the pathway to freedom from bitterness and pain.

If you're not already, someday you may be a parent. Be a role model and treat your parents and grandparents today the way you hope to be treated by your children and grandchildren in the future.

DRAFT DAY

Bam saw how dedicated his mother was to him, and he remained dedicated to taking care of her to thank her for all her hard work and positive influence in his life. He saw her love for him, and he wanted to give back.

You might not be in the financial position Bam was in, but parents don't always want money or presents from their kids. Sometimes they only want to know they are loved.

As I mentioned earlier, forgive them if they have done something to hurt or wrong you. That might be tough, but it's worth the self-examination.

Show them respect and honor. If you are a student of Scripture, in Exodus, you are advised to "honor thy father and thy mother; that thy days may be long upon the land which the Lord thy God giveth thee."

Do your best to respect their position, even when they disappoint you.

Always do your best to speak well of them to others and carry on a solid reputation. If you are in a circumstance where your heritage was damaged, make a fresh start to bring honor to the family tree.

Never be ashamed of who you are in life.

Lift them up in public and in private. As a parent, I want my kids to let me know they love me regardless of where we are. I would much rather hear them tell me they love me in my own home than in front of an audience. But I'll take both.

Another way to honor your parents or grandparents is to seek their wisdom. Life is the best instructor, and they have been through life's twists and turns. They have many years of experience and can offer sound advice. Ask for their insight and opinions.

Show them support for all they have done for you. This is not payback time, but you should not pass up an opportunity to let them know they are appreciated.

Some parents live alone, and the thing they want the most is for their son or daughter to visit them. Don't just check in on the holidays. If you live far away, use technology and video chat with them on a regular basis.

If needed, you can also provide financial support if you are in a position to do so.

Do your best to honor your parents. You will want your children to do the same, so set the example. If your children see you respect your parents, they will likely return the favor.

Be the bigger person. Give credit and thanks when they are due; don't wait until it's too late.

Go Big Blue!

How can you show your parents or grandparents more love?

WEEK 41 | THE FOX AND THE BRUIN

WHAT HAPPENS WHEN THE TWO best point guards in the nation meet in a head-to-head matchup?

What if the two point guards play for two of the most storied programs in college basketball?

What if the two storied programs are then scheduled to meet in a titanic matchup in the Sweet Sixteen of the NCAA tournament?

What if the matchup is also a winner-take-all rematch of an intensely played contest from earlier in the year?

What if I told you the dad of one of the point guards has been running his mouth with some brashly worded quotes?

Take all that intrigue, and you've got number-two Kentucky versus number-three UCLA on Friday, March 24, 2017—*that's what!* The irresistible force meeting the immovable object. De'Aaron Fox and Lonzo Ball leading their respective teams in the Round of Sixteen in the Big Dance in Memphis. If that wasn't enough, it also just so happens to be a revenge game of sorts for the Big Blue—for the 97–92 homecourt thumping the Bruins handed them at Rupp earlier in the year. Throw in LeVar Ball proclaiming Kentucky as just "a tune-up" for his son's Final Four appearance, and you can see why it was one of the most anticipated battles in tournament history.

LeVar Ball was "that dad" on steroids. With a trio of uber-talented sons, he went out of his way to promote all of them in the most outlandish manner possible. Part carnival barker and part hype man, his goal was to make sure everybody in the basketball world and beyond knew his sons were NBA worthy.

Number-one son Lonzo Ball was already draft lottery material. In the meeting with Kentucky earlier in the year, Lonzo did it all. He finished with 14 points, 7 assists, and 6 rebounds as his eleventh-ranked team controlled the game throughout and snapped number-one-ranked Kentucky's forty-two-game home winning streak in the surprising upset victory. In a game in which "defense was optional," Fox held his own—scoring 20 points and dishing out 9 assists in the losing effort.

Now, with an Elite Eight birth at stake, the two teams would go at it again—with the world expecting an epic showdown as LeVar continued to spew superlatives about his son.

However, in this survive-and-advance rematch, it was Fox who let his game do the talking—scoring a career-high and freshman NCAA tournament single game record of 39 points. With a chip on his shoulder and the skills to match, Fox got the best of Lonzo by far—scoring in bunches and drawing fouls in every way imaginable—as Kentucky secured the highly rewarding 86–75 win.

For the evening, Fox shot 13 of 20 from the field and made 13 of 15 from the foul line. Just as impressively, he held Ball to 10 points on 4 of 10 shooting. Kentucky, meanwhile, slowed the pace—intermittently mucking up the game in order to disrupt the high-powered Bruin offense while making UCLA work tirelessly on the defensive end of the court.

In the 2017 NBA draft, both Fox and Ball were selected in the first round—Ball at number two by the Los Angeles Lakers and Fox at number five by the Sacramento Kings. Although they're both in the midst of successful professional careers,

Kentucky fans will primarily remember that one matchup between them—the time that the Fox schooled the Bruin in their classic NCAA tournament showdown.

SCOUTING REPORT

You've been there. We have all been at a sporting event, at work, or maybe even at family gatherings around the blustery loudmouth who knows everything. Let's hope it's not you, but if it is, keep reading.

Competition is good in business, in sports, in life.

Confidence is also good in business, in sports, in life.

But cockiness and arrogance are not good in any of these areas. Sooner or later, harsh words will come back to haunt you.

Words can motivate and inspire. They can build up and tear down.

They can make for a friendly competition or be used as a means of revenge.

But overall, competition is a positive thing.

Have you been on the receiving end of someone's loud blathering? Or perhaps you've been the one doing it. No one enjoys being around "that parent" who thinks their kid is the best.

When you are ready to go into battle, the last thing you need is for someone to stoke the fire.

What brings out the best in you? Have you been up against another person for a job promotion and your competition boasts to you about their chances? Or maybe a heated exchange of words takes place during a sporting event.

THE MATCHUP

Don't back down or be afraid to compete. And don't be the one who runs your mouth when you may not be able to back up what you say.

Win with humility and lose with class and dignity, even if your opponent does not show the same sportsmanship.

True competition lets you know where you stand on the court. It will elevate your talents and expose your weaknesses. It will help you sharpen your skills and focus on your will to win.

Don't ever expect your wins in life to be handed to you. Only the victories you earn will be meaningful to you.

Go out and practice hard and expect to be triumphant. Never expect an easy win.

Prepare diligently for that intense interview for a new career. Go the extra mile and put together a memorable portfolio that will knock the socks off your potential employer.

Competition is a good thing.

If you are not a part of the game, it's fine to cheer for the players on the court, but don't be "that parent" who brings humiliation and embarrassment to everyone involved. LeVar Ball learned a tough lesson and had egg on his face after his son's loss.

How hard do you compete?

Do you run your mouth when you shouldn't? How can you be a graceful champion?

_____

_____

_____

_____

_____

_____

_____

_____

WEEK 42 | TWIN TOWERS

A LONG TIME AGO IN a galaxy far, far away . . . big men actually dominated the sport of college basketball. Recruit one commanding center to control the paint, and your team would automatically become a title contender. If you somehow got two "aircraft carriers" on scholarship, you'd better start enlarging your trophy case.

Mike Phillips and Rick Robey were the first two "twin towers" to grace the hardwood together at Rupp Arena. Phillips and Robey—both listed as 6'10" and 235 pounds—could score, rebound, and set picks that would knock your molars loose. Any opponents attempting to drive the lane would do so at their own risk. "King and Kong"—as they were affectionately known within the BBN—were instrumental cogs in bringing home the 1978 championship trophy.

A few years later, Kentucky Basketball would be introduced to another set of "twin towers." Sam Bowie and Melvin Turpin were big men who had a unique set of skills. Turpin was a seven-footer out of Lexington's Bryan Station High School who had a deft shooting touch. Give him the ball within fifteen feet of the basket, and his turnaround jump shot could find the bottom of the net every time. One night in Knoxville, he put 42 points on the defenseless Vols. If not for the problems with his appetite and weight, Turpin would have eventually taken the NBA by storm.

Sam Bowie had big-man skills that were even more extraordinary. At 7'1" with the speed and agility of a gazelle, the guy could outrun and outjump any mortal man assigned to defend him. Coming out of Lebanon High School in Pennsylvania, Sam was hot stuff . . . and he acted like he knew it from the opening tip. When Sam committed to Kentucky, the Wildcats were also just a smidgeon away from getting Ralph Sampson—another 7'4" prodigy out of Virginia. Sampson made a last-second decision to sign with the home-state Cavaliers, so that opened up the way for the Bowie/Turpin combo.

Unfortunately, Sam developed a stress fracture in his left tibia after his sophomore year. He would sit out two seasons waiting for his leg to recover. Although he made it back for the 1983–1984 season, he was never really the same from that point on. Still, when he and Turpin teamed up in the frontcourt, it always made for some pretty interesting theater.

Sunday, January 22, 1984, is a date UK fans will remember. Besides it being Super Bowl Sunday between the Redskins and the Raiders, that was the day that Hakeem Olajuwon of Houston paid a visit to the 23,992 onlookers at Rupp Arena. "Akeem the Dream"—as he was aptly nicknamed—could score, rebound, and defend. Considered one of the greatest basketball players of all time, the seven-footer from Nigeria was selected ahead of both Bowie and Michael Jordan in the 1984 NBA draft.

But on this particular afternoon, Kentucky had two big men to Houston's one. Houston would jump out to an 11–1 lead, but Roger Harden provided a big spark off the bench, and Kentucky battled back for a 35–31 halftime lead. In the second stanza, the Cats stretched the lead out to 61–51 with just under eight minutes to play. Houston would make one final run, cutting the lead to three, before Kentucky eventually prevailed.

Olajuwon was "held" to only 14 points, 12 rebounds, and 5 blocked shots before fouling out with 6:14 left in the game. Bowie had only 8 points himself—but managed to pull down 18 boards and had 2 blocked shots in the process. Turpin, meanwhile, scorched the stat sheets with 19 points, 11 rebounds, and 2 blocks of his own.

Statistics, however, don't tell the whole story of that 74–67 Wildcat victory. It was the titanic battle under the backboard that fans will always remember. There were fingerprints all over the glass at the end of that day. Although it happened a long time ago in what seemed a galaxy a world away, it was still an incredibly special Sunday for Kentucky's "twin towers."

SCOUTING TRIP

Some people hesitate to have lofty goals because of their fear of failure.

They may be content to go through the motions and settle for less. They choose the comfort zone because it is a safe place that never disappoints you.

Are you afraid to have big dreams—all-star seven-footer-type dreams?

How about coming up with a backup plan just in case? This doesn't mean you won't be successful, but it can be reassuring to have two plans, or "twin towers"—just like the Cats did.

If you are going to have a dream, it might as well be *big*. Just make sure it's attainable and within reach.

You can aspire to hit your goals and raise your banner, but it will not come easy.

Dream for something new in your life and have the ambition to go for it with excitement and anticipation.

Will your dreams come true? You won't find out without trying.

MAKE THE COMMITMENT

When you dream big, you will find out what you're really made of.

If you want a certain career, your challenge might be attending college for several years. This is a sacrifice and commitment that takes true dedication.

When you dream big, you move beyond your current situation and plan for a brighter tomorrow. It means you are not settling for the current moment but instead setting your sights on something bigger.

In your quest to achieve your dreams, you will develop new habits that will prove to be useful throughout your life.

You will be able to expand your network of people who will inspire you to work hard.

Working toward your goals will also teach you how to deal with success and failure. You may have setbacks, but when you fall down, get back up and try again. Perhaps you won't succeed. Or you might become more than you ever imagined.

Having a dream is a wonderful thing. Make it realistic and attainable.

Then shoot the lights out in your championship game.

Go Big Blue!

How can you chase your dreams? What obstacles will you face?

WEEK 43 | BLOCKED

THERE'S NOTHING MORE DEMORALIZING THAN getting blocked. I'm not talking about your social media account either. I'm talking about getting your shot swatted away on the basketball court—rejected into the third row as you're driving down the lane for the winning basket.

Kentucky has had its fair share of shot blockers through the years. Jamaal Magloire is the all-time career leader with 268. Of course, he played four full years at UK. Willie Cauley-Stein—who played three seasons—checks in at number two with 233 rejections to his credit. Other preeminent Wildcat shot blockers over the years include Melvin Turpin (226), Sam Bowie (218), and Andre Riddick (212).

Anthony Davis sits at the top of the list for the most blocks per game during a single season (186). Every Wildcat fan remembers his rejection of North Carolina's John Henson's potential game winner on December 3, 2011, in Rupp Arena. Reggie Bullock had just hit a three-pointer for the fifth-ranked Tar Heels to cut number-one-ranked Kentucky's lead to 73–72 with forty-eight seconds left. After freshman Marquis Teague missed the front end of the bonus, Davis blocked Henson's shot and grabbed the rebound, and the Cats ran out the clock to preserve the victory.

We all know what happened to Anthony Davis. He went on to become one of the most decorated Wildcat heroes of all time. His ability to do the things other than score—like blocking shots—helped lead Kentucky to their eighth national championship while making Davis one of the most popular UK players ever.

The Kentucky record for the most blocked shots in a single game is twelve. That distinction belongs to Nerlens Noel, a 6'10" shot-blocking machine from Everett, Massachusetts. It happened on January 29, 2013, at the Tad Pad in Oxford, Mississippi. Noel, who scored only 2 points that evening, more than made up for it on the defensive end of the court with his 7-rebound, 12-block performance. Kyle Wiltjer and Archie Goodwin led Kentucky in scoring with 26 and 24 points, respectively, as the unranked Wildcats upset the sixteenth-ranked Rebels 87–74.

Unfortunately for Noel and the BBN, Nerlens's season ended four games later down in the Stephen C. O'Connell Center in Gainesville, Florida. While attempting to chase down and block a layup attempt by the Gators' Mike Rosario, Noel ran smack-dab into the basketball support, banged his left knee, and tore his ACL in the process. The O'Dome is known for being rather compacted around the playing court, so you have to wonder if the tight setup somehow contributed to the devastating injury.

That injury not only put an end to Nerlens's college career but also derailed Kentucky's season. Without their backboard eraser in the middle, the Wildcats went on to an unremarkable 21–12 record while suffering an embarrassing 59–57 season-ending loss to Robert Morris in the NIT.

Despite not finishing out the full season, Noel was still selected as the 2012–2013 SEC Freshman of the Year and the SEC Defensive Player of the Year. He also made First Team All-SEC as well as the All-SEC Freshman Team. Noel was drafted number six overall in the first round of the 2013 NBA draft by the New Orleans Pelicans.

Kentucky fans will always remember 2013 as the year Nerlens Noel went down with the injury. And without Nerlens blocking shots, the Wildcats were blocked from the NCAA tournament.

AFTER THE BLOCK

A pivotal block in a game can inspire one side and demoralize the other.

Have you ever been driving to score and get off a shot that is sure to bank off the board and go through the hoop for 2 points and the win? Then, out of nowhere, your shot gets launched into the fifth row. You are stunned and feel like you let your team down.

Has this ever happened to you in real life?

You thought you were going to get that job offer to help you get out of debt. Or you were counting on a promotion that would finally acknowledge your hard work.

Being passed over or told no does and will happen. "You are not the right fit at this time" and "We need a person with more experience" are phrases that can discourage you more than a blocked shot ever can. These phrases can send the message that you are not qualified, and many times you might take it as a personal rejection. You are not good enough.

Rejection is a part of life. There is no way around it.

When this happens, you have two options: let it destroy you, or use it to make you stronger.

GO IN FOR THE DUNK

When you open that email containing the rejection notice, you must realize it's a part of life. I have experienced plenty of rejections. It stings for a bit, but you have to let it pass.

It's okay to be discouraged for a few hours or a couple of days. But you must drive to the hoop and keep shooting.

Just because one person told you no does not mean everyone will. Most fishers don't catch a fish on their first cast. The more lines you throw in the water, the better your chances are of making that big catch.

When you are rejected, seek comfort in friends and family, and express your feelings to those who you trust to listen.

Try to stay busy with activities and keep your mind off the situation.

Take time to examine why you were told no. Look for areas where you can improve and be flexible enough to make changes for the better.

But keep going. Don't give up.

The rejection you received means you are one step closer to an acceptance.

Mark Amend once said, "Rejection doesn't mean you aren't good enough; it means the other person failed to notice what you have to offer."

Go Cats!

How can you handle rejection?

How will you drive to the hole again?

_____

_____

_____

_____

_____

_____

_____

WEEK 44 | FIVE-STAR SURPRISES

TWO OF THE BIGGEST KENTUCKY Basketball success stories involved players from whom not a whole lot was expected. Sadly, you won't find many of those stories anymore in today's one-and-done culture. Unless you're a five-star recruit—or else have some Kentucky ties à la Dominique Hawkins or Derek Willis—chances are you'll be applying your talents at someplace other than the University of Kentucky. That's just the nature of the current beast.

Occasionally, though, someone might end up sneaking into the Kentucky camp with less-than-stellar high school credentials. That most recent someone was Shai Gilgeous-Alexander. The 6'5" combo guard from Hamilton, Ontario, was considered by the experts as—at best—a four-star recruit with a limited ceiling.

While his future UK five-star teammates (Quade Green, P. J. Washington, Jarred Vanderbilt, and Nick Richards) were plying their trades at the prestigious Jordan Brand Classic high school all-star game at Madison Square Garden, Gilgeous-Alexander was relegated to a second-rate appearance at the local Derby Classic event in Louisville. Although he dazzled the fans in attendance that evening, few thought he would become an impact player at UK—especially among his more highly heralded teammates.

Boy, were they wrong! Not only did Shai hang with his team-mates; he quickly surpassed them. Armed with a huge heart and a work ethic to match, Gilgeous-Alexander somehow worked himself into the starting rotation. From there, a 30-point game on January 30, 2018, in an 83–80 overtime thriller against Vanderbilt followed. Then, on February 28, came a 17-point, 10-assist, 7-rebound monster of a game in a 96–78 rout of Mississippi. In the SEC championship game in St. Louis that year, Shai led Kentucky to a 77–72 victory over Tennessee with a gargantuan 29-point, 7-rebound, 3-assist, 2-steal effort. Before you knew it, Shai was selected to the All-SEC Freshman Team, made the All-SEC Second Team, and was the SEC Tournament MVP.

At the conclusion of his heck-of-a-surprising season, Shai became a lottery pick in the 2018 NBA draft—selected number eleven overall by the Charlotte Hornets.

Compared to Shai Gilgeous-Alexander, Nazr Mohammed was even more unheralded coming out of high school. Even his coach at Chicago's Kenwood Academy wondered why Rick Pitino had any interest in the 6'10" 315-pound overweight behemoth. Mohammed was—at best—a project relegated to another warm body in practice or perhaps five additional fouls off the bench when a hatchet man was called for.

Pitino and Mohammed, however, had other ideas. Pitino's vaunted conditioning program, supplemented by strict nutritional guidelines, quickly worked its magic. Nazr lost thirty pounds his freshman year, and by the 1997–1998 season, he had trimmed down to a svelte 240 pounds and was the leading rebounder and second-leading scorer on a team that would go on to win the school's seventh national title.

Mohammed may be best remembered for his last-second heroics on January 27, 1998, on the road at Vanderbilt. With less than a second to go on the clock in Memorial Gymnasium, he somehow managed to throw up an impossible scoop shot that gave the seventh-ranked Wildcats an improbable 63–61 victory over the hard-luck Commodores.

Just like Shai Gilgeous-Alexander, Nazr Mohammed also wound up as a first-round selection in the NBA draft—selected number twenty-nine overall in 1998 by the Utah Jazz. Even more incredibly, Nazr would play in the league for the next eighteen straight years.

It just goes to show you that even at Kentucky, you don't have to be a five-star prodigy to rise to the top and enjoy success. Can anyone say Tyler Herro?

LOW PRESEASON POLL

Sometimes circumstances in your life that are out of your control might affect how people view you.

That's unfortunate, but it's reality. If you grew up in a poor household, this may have placed a stigma on you. Those who are raised in poverty or are part of a broken home often have to work much harder than others to overcome challenges and achieve success.

Your reputation is very much linked to your family heritage. While you can definitely break from your upbringing and change your story, it takes persistence, dedication, and hard work.

Sometimes you are to blame for how others perceive you due to mistakes you have made in the past. A reputation of having an upstanding character and integrity that took a lifetime to build can vanish in a moment and take years to recoup, and it might never be fully restored.

Has this happened to you?

Have you played in the shadows of others with the knowledge you could excel if you just got the chance?

BE A FIVE-STAR RECRUIT

Reputation matters, and it's earned. At least it should be.

What others think of you can affect your job, your relationships, and how you fit in to society.

Everyone can make wrong choices. And, if regret is demonstrated with a desire to learn, everyone deserves a second chance. Or at least a chance to start over.

It begins with knowing who you are and not being concerned with how others define you.

A reputation takes a long time to earn, and it can be destroyed in minutes.

Owning up to a mistake is the first key.

The second is noticing your potential. You have your own special gifts and talents. If you don't know what they are yet, keep searching and be patient.

Someone will notice someday. Shai Gilgeous-Alexander, Nazr Mohammed, and Tyler Herro all received the opportunity to prove themselves, and their UK careers are forever etched in BBN history.

Keep being true to yourself and others and work hard toward your goal.

Believe in who you are. If changes are needed, make them. Go back to school or get in shape. If you don't take the first step to make improvements, how do you expect others to notice you?

Humble yourself, and step forward with confidence.

Your biggest adjustment might be developing an attitude of gratitude. You may not be in the ideal situation yet but be thankful for what you have today. Once you appreciate your current circumstances, you can look to the future and be happy with who God made you to be in life.

Go Big Blue!

What defines you? What changes can you make?

WEEK 45 | NOTHING SUCKS LIKE A BIG ORANGE

BEFORE THERE WAS A LAETTNER shot, a Dean Dome, candy-striped warm-up pants, or any sort of "L's Down," there was Kentucky's all-out basketball rivalry with Tennessee. For those of us old enough to remember, you know this was more than just a spirited game of hoops. This was the basketball equivalent of the Hatfields and McCoys.

This particular border war featured a ghastly cast of unlikeable characters. UT coach Ray Mears—clad in that hideous orange blazer with a unicycle at the ready—was public enemy number one. He was Bruce Pearl before Bruce Pearl. As Wildcat fans quickly learned, the guy was a master showman, but he could also coach. For fifteen years he dared to challenge the supremacy of the Big Blue by playing them dead even.

The Bernie and Ernie Show was a virtual horrorfest for BBN. Bernard King could score on anyone, while Ernie Grunfeld could cheat with the best of them. Let's never forget the glamour-guzzling Grunfeld intentionally stepping to the charity stripe to shoot free throws to beat Kentucky when he wasn't even the player who was fouled.

And what about Stokely Athletic Center—the Vols' old home court? Talk about nightmares. The place was ancient and decrepit—more like a drafty airplane hangar than a sports gymnasium. That first UK versus U of L dream game was held in Stokely during the 1983 NCAA Mideast regionals. Everyone remembers Jim Master hitting the shot to tie the game in regulation. We won't talk about what happened in overtime.

Speaking of bad memories, how about Dale Ellis? Or Ballard High School's own Allan Houston defecting to the Vols? Or, worse yet, Mason County's Chris Lofton? The kid could shoot like no other—and yes, Tubby should have signed him at the outset. How about Scotty Hopson from Hopkinsville, or Ron Slay's headband, or Jarnell Stokes—who's still probably figuring out how to stretch? Don DeVoe, Tony White, Howard Wood, Admiral Schofield, flopping Grant Williams, and Smokey the Dog—the list of orange-clad tormentors goes on and on.

It hasn't, however, always been gloom and doom against the Vols. Remember the night of January 31, 1983, when Melvin Turpin put up 42 points against a woebegone Tennessee defense. The Big Dipper couldn't miss, hitting 18 of 22 shots from the floor and grabbing 12 rebounds. It was a magical evening, even though Tennessee somehow pulled off the upset.

But Wildcat fans have had more than their fair share of victories in this rivalry. Kentucky's 101–40 thrashing of Tennessee—on March 12 in the 1993 SEC tournament held at Rupp Arena—had to be some kind of record, right? Thirteen SEC tournament records at the time to be exact, including the most points scored (101), three-point shots made (12), assists (30), steals (19), opponent turnovers (30), and opponent's lowest field-goal percentage (23.1%).

Or who can forget January 14, 2009, in Thompson-Boling Arena? That was the night Jodie Meeks went off—shooting 15 of 22 from the field and 14 of 14 from the foul line—setting the Kentucky single-game scoring record of 54 points.

Hey, even Billy Gillispie beat Tennessee. Enough said!

Nothing sucks like a Big Orange!

THE HOSTILE ENVIRONMENT

Remember going into that gym to play your biggest rival in the conference? I can recall when my son played on a travel team that went deep into the hills of West Virginia for a tournament. It got ugly. The host fans were not pleased when we won the title on their court, and our coach told the boys to go straight to the bus after the game. He sent assistant coaches and some dads into the locker room to gather the players' gear and clothes. It was that bad.

How do you handle rivals or confrontation at home or at work? Most don't enjoy it, but there are some who actually thrive on tension.

When tempers get the best of a person, it can lead to an uncomfortable environment.

But unfortunately, it's a part of life that must sometimes be addressed. Perhaps you have a strained relationship at home with family members, or maybe one of your coworkers is unbearable to be around.

No matter what is causing it, tension can make you feel sick to your stomach.

JUMP BALL

You cannot let someone roll over you or make you feel uneasy or afraid. There are some ways to handle these situations without coming off as obnoxious or a coward.

Sometimes the best way to handle controversy is to simply avoid it. But when you are forced into confrontation, consider the following ways to meet the problem head-on without fear.

Try to prepare mentally and evaluate what and how you are thinking and feeling before you face the moment. Put your emotions aside and focus on the issues that are relevant or essential to the discussion.

Then try to set the stage for yourself to play on your home court. Conflict does not mean you have to engage in a fight. Don't make a scene in public or cause a disturbance. A private discussion is always best; having a witness is also wise.

A healthy, productive discussion should always be the goal. Yelling and screaming do not solve anything. If you are upset with your children or parents, take a few minutes to calm down before addressing the situation. Maybe you are upset that your boss didn't give you a promotion. Collect your thoughts, put your talking points together, and schedule an appointment to engage in a discussion about what you can do to qualify for the next opportunity. Work together to identify the issues and find a way to solve the problem.

You must be the one who believes in a mutually satisfying resolution. Lead the way and set the example.

Rivalries and competition in the game of basketball can be fun and generate excitement. Players learn to sharpen their skills and practice harder to get the big win. But in real life, constant clashes can be exhausting and unproductive.

Be the bigger person. Unless, of course, you are Jodie Meeks. Go Big Blue Nation!

How can you settle a dispute at home or at work?

What can you do to ease any tension?

_____

_____

_____

_____

_____

_____

WEEK 46 | IT'S ALL ABOUT THE WINS

THERE'S ANOTHER IMPORTANT UK RECORD that most likely will never be broken. It's the all-time career total of 131 wins held by Wayne Turner.

First of all, to break the record, someone would have to play at least four full years for the Blue and White. In this one-and-done culture, anybody who's any good won't stick around anywhere near that amount of time. Turner played before the one-and-done era, logging minutes in 151 of the 152 games UK played in his four seasons in Lexington.

Second, your team also has to be fairly good to advance far enough in the tournament for you to accumulate all those extra games on your résumé. Turner's teams were pretty darn good—advancing to the SEC championship in all four of the years he played and the NCAA tournament finals in three of his four years.

And finally, you have to be fairly skilled and amazingly durable to average nearly thirty-eight games a year for all four years that you're in school. Turner checked both of those boxes, scoring 1,170 total points and dishing out 494 assists while remaining virtually injury free. With his wiry build and hitch in his jump shot, it's easy to forget how good and steady Turner actually was.

One thing UK fans won't ever forget is Turner taking Duke's Steve Wojciechowski to school in that 1998 NCAA South regional final in Tampa—when Wayne repeatedly beat Wojo down the lane to either score or dish to an open teammate. Not only did Kentucky rally from a 17-point deficit to beat the Blue Devils that afternoon, but they also went on to win their seventh national championship a week later.

Wayne Turner also remains UK's all-time career steals leader with an astonishing 238 thefts to his credit. He's also tied with Rajon Rondo for the most steals in a game (8). That happened on November 24, 1997, at the Maui Classic Invitational held in Lahaina, Hawaii. In a game where the rest of the team was ice-cold, Turner shot 6 of 11 from the field to lead all scorers with 16 points as Kentucky defeated George Washington 70–55.

The Maui Classic was one early-season trip Kentucky fans always looked forward to. Regardless of the opposition, Cat fans regarded it as a badge of honor to pack the tiny court in the Lahaina Civic Center. It didn't matter that they just spent thousands of dollars to be surrounded by sun, sea, sand, and surf, the Big Blue faithful were proud to support their C-A-Y-U-T-S in a stuffy gymnasium 4,500 miles from home.

One memorable Kentucky Basketball image came directly out of Maui several years before Turner's record-setting game. It took place against Arizona on December 23, 1993, in the championship contest. With just 5.5 seconds left in the game, Arizona's Khalid Reeves sank two free throws to give his thirteenth-ranked Wildcats a 92–91 lead over fifth-ranked Kentucky. Kentucky then pushed the ball down the court to Rodrick Rhodes, who missed a deep three from the right wing. Jeff Brassow charged in under the left side of the goal, somehow got his hand on the errant carom, and guided the miss off the glass and into the bucket just milliseconds ahead of the final buzzer.

The image of Rick Pitino dancing with joy in a celebratory, hug-filled saunter remains indelibly etched in the minds of everyone who witnessed it.

It's all about the wins—especially when they take place in paradise. BBN misses Maui!

THE STRATEGY SESSIONS

One of a gazillion reasons Kentucky Basketball has been successful over the years is its consistency.

They have a model and tradition of winning comparable to none. No other program in college basketball is as celebrated as BBN.

Kentucky Basketball wins no matter who is on the court or who is coaching. It's expected.

What's expected of you? Do you always give your best effort? Do you exhibit a positive attitude and promote teamwork?

If you are lacking in any of these traits, call a time-out and regroup. Life can be stressful and difficult at times, but it's up to you to prevail.

Winning can be a lot of pressure. This is why a coach on the sidelines loses their cool once in a while and may earn a technical foul. Blowing off steam does not get you tossed out of life's game, but it detracts from your focus.

When you are calm, consistent, and dependable, you can lead your team to victory.

THE WINNING STREAK

One of the best tips to playing all four quarters in your daily life is to follow a routine.

Consistency is a blessing.

Wake up with a positive attitude and begin the day with a motivational or devotional book for inspiration. Set your alarm for the same time each day, get up, and be ready to greet the world.

Set your sights on doing good, and don't let anyone talk you out of it. When you don't feel like doing a good deed, shake it off and get busy.

Be effective. Be encouraging. Set the example.

Take responsibility for your progress, and don't make excuses when you lose a game. Simply examine what went wrong and make changes so you have different results next time.

You will take bad shots in life and make some wrong decisions. Own up to them and learn to do better.

When you focus on activities and goals that make you happy, it's easier to stick with the program. When you wake up to a life you enjoy, you tend to want to do what is right.

Release any negative thoughts and recognize how far you have come in your journey.

John Wayne once said that "looking back is a bad habit." Focus on the present and the future.

When you follow some of these suggestions, you might find it easier to stay on track and be consistent in life. Consistency is a key to winning.

Go Cats!

How can you demonstrate longevity? How can you keep winning?

_____

_____

_____

WEEK 47 | OH SO CLOSE!

WHAT ARE THE TOP THREE heart-rending losses in Kentucky Basketball history? It depends on who you ask, but number one on the list for nearly all of BBN has to be the Laettner shot in '92.

Most Wildcat fans would rank the 2015 Wisconsin loss as a close second. After all, Kentucky was 38–0 going into that game and on a collision course with hoops destiny.

Coming in at number three might just be the loss to Texas Western in the '66 national championship game.

The date was March 19, 1966. Kentucky, ranked number one at the time, was a heavy favorite to win title number five. Texas Western, however, had other plans. Bobby Joe Hill scored 20 points, and the third-ranked Miners used an aggressive ball-hawking defense to pull off the 72–65 upset before a crowd of 14,253 at Cole Field House in College Park, Maryland. The Cats fell behind at the midway point of the first half, battled back valiantly to within a point, but just couldn't overtake the bigger, flashier Don Haskins–coached team from El Paso.

Pat Riley and Louie Dampier scored 19 points apiece to lead Kentucky—a team aptly named "Rupp's Runts" because they boasted no starter taller than 6'5". Together with Thad Jaracz, Tommy Kron, and Larry Conley—Riley, Dampier, and the rest of the Runts had endeared themselves to UK fans because of their hustle, grit, and ability to put the ball in the basket.

Louie Dampier could certainly put the ball in the basket. The six-foot-nuthin' guard from Indianapolis was one of the purest shooters to ever wear the Kentucky uniform. During his three seasons playing for the Blue and White, Dampier shot over 50 percent from the field—most of them bombs from long range before the advent of the three-point line. His 1,575 total career points still ranks him twelfth on UK's all-time scoring list.

"We were all crushed," Dampier said, reflecting on the aftermath of the Texas Western loss many years later. "It was the first time that I had ever seen Coach Rupp upset—really sad about it. Usually he'd come in as his strong self and holler at us for losing the game and get on us for different things . . . but he was just meekly quiet."

During his time at UK, Dampier was a three-time All-SEC selection and a two-time All-American. He also ranks as one of the nicest, most humble former players to ever walk the earth.

Dampier continued his magical scoring touch in the professional ranks. He played nine seasons with the Kentucky Colonels of the ABA and three additional years in the NBA with the San Antonio Spurs. He holds the ABA record for points scored (13,726), three-pointers (794), assists (4,044), games played (728), and minutes played (27,770). In 2015, he joined ex-UK players C. M. Newton, Cliff Hagan, Frank Ramsey, Adrian Smith, Pat Riley, and Dan Issel as a fellow inductee into the prestigious Naismith Basketball Hall of Fame.

Not bad for a 6'0" runt. Louie did it all. The only thing missing is a UK championship ring on his finger.

THE LETDOWN LOSS

Losing a game is not fun but brace yourself because it will happen. How you deal with it reveals a lot about your personality and character.

You never have to like a defeat or a setback, but you must accept the outcome and plan a strategy to come back for the next contest.

Winston Churchill said, "Success is not final, failure is not fatal: it is the courage to continue that counts."

A win is only as good as the moment, but a loss can teach a lesson for a lifetime.

Maybe you have experienced a loss. Disappointments happen each day. But it's how you rebound that defines you.

Perhaps you lost a job after you followed the rules and did everything you were asked to do and more. Or maybe you've been devasted by the end of a personal relationship you thought was rock-solid.

Or maybe you or a loved one are going through a health crisis that has had an impact on your mental toughness as well as your finances.

THE PEP TALK

Zig Ziglar once said, "It's not how far you fall but how high you bounce that counts."

Disappointments and failures are bound to happen. They can be difficult to deal with and pose different challenges.

If life knocks you down and your happiness is in jeopardy, how will you respond?

Will you face the truth or try to justify your situation and make excuses?

When life comes at you and power dunks on your dreams and ambitions, it can be tough. You might feel dejected and embarrassed. Acknowledge when this happens, then pick yourself up off the court and keep playing.

Don't dwell on the past because it can consume you and invite bitterness.

Playing the victim card also does not help the situation. No matter what has happened, use your skills and knowledge to move forward.

If you are taken advantage of, speak up or just walk away.

Never engage in a hostile situation, but do be prepared to defend yourself.

Reexamine your goals to see if they are reachable. Life does not offer guarantees, and you might have to adjust your expectations accordingly.

Weigh the pros and cons and go after your goals with eyes wide open.

Always look for the positive, and don't let yourself get dragged down by the negative. Take time to be kind to yourself, especially when things don't work out as planned. You may be turned down for a job if you're not the best match for a company's needs. Look for a different one. The person you are attracted to may not return your affections. Find someone who will.

It's important to look at the situation to see what you can learn. Adopt a compassionate attitude, and don't judge yourself harshly. You do not want to get stuck in shame.

And finally, be willing to adapt and try something new.

"Insanity is doing the same thing over and over again and expecting different results," said Albert Einstein.

Disappointments will happen. It's up to you to overcome them.

Go Big Blue!

How can you overcome?

_____

_____

_____

WEEK 48 | MISSED IT BY THAT MUCH

THERE'S ONLY BEEN ONE TEAM in the history of college basketball that has started its season 38–0. Yep, you guessed it—it's the University of Kentucky.

Already off to the best start in school and SEC history, that 2014–2015 version of the Wildcats ended the regular season with a 67–50 thumping of the Florida Gators. With that perfect 31–0 record intact, the Wildcats became the first team from a power five conference to go undefeated in the regular season since Indiana did so in 1976. It was also the fifteenth time the Cats went undefeated in the conference, setting a Rupp Arena record that year with nineteen home wins in the process.

One of the stars of that team was Karl Anthony-Towns. "KAT" —as he came to be known by BBN—was a 6'11" 250-pound basketball prodigy from New Jersey. His mother was Dominican, so Towns was selected at the ripe old age of sixteen to play on the Dominican Republic National Basketball team in 2012. John Calipari just happened to be coaching the Dominican team at the time, and that relationship with his star player led naturally to Towns winding up at Kentucky.

KAT's one-and-done year with the Big Blue just happened to be the year of Calipari's infamous "platoon" system. Having to share minutes with nine other talented teammates subsequently limited his statistical output. Towns's rather pedestrian

10.3 points per game and 6.7 rebounds belied his true value and effectiveness on a team that excelled when he exerted his dominance in the paint.

Nowhere was that dominance more evident—and needed—than against Notre Dame in the NCAA tournament. The date was March 28, 2015. Nearly twenty thousand fans were packed into Quicken Loans Arena in Cleveland, Ohio, for the Midwest regional matchup between top-ranked Kentucky and the eighth-ranked Irish. The Wildcats had just come off of a 78–39 thrashing of Bob Huggins's West Virginia team after the Mountaineers ran their mouths. Confidence was high as the Cats looked to advance to another Final Four on their march to another potential national championship.

The Fighting Irish proved tougher than initially thought. They controlled the tempo from the outset and held a 6-point lead—the game's largest—well into the second half. With less than four and a half minutes left in the contest, Mike Brey's team still led by 4. But with just 1:14 remaining, Towns tied the game on a layup. Andrew Harrison made two free throws with six seconds left on the clock, and Willie Cauley-Stein made a fantastic defensive stop running the length of the court to seal the 68–66 heart-stopping victory as the buzzer sounded.

For the night, Towns led all scorers with 25 points on 10 of 13 shooting. He was virtually automatic in the second half, taking 8 shots without a miss. Time after time, Kentucky fed the ball to their go-to guy down low, and he delivered on every single possession.

After the season, Towns was selected as a consensus All-American. He also made All-SEC and the All-SEC Freshman Team and was the SEC Freshman of the Year. The Minnesota Timberwolves picked him as the number-one overall player in the 2015 NBA draft.

Unfortunately, Towns's UK team fell just short of a fairy-tale ending, losing 71–64 to Wisconsin on a blown call for a shot clock violation in the Final Four semifinals. Kentucky fans still lament about what could have been. But that shouldn't detract from how good that 2015 Kentucky team was, what they accomplished during the season, and how close they actually came to becoming a team of destiny.

THE FINAL SCORE

Winning is the best. The fanfare. A job well done. Mission accomplished.

But we don't always win in life.

You can be scooting along in your journey and doing everything right and playing by the rules. Then just when you least expect it, the other team knocks you off your pedestal.

All that work. All that sacrifice. Poof. Gone.

What's left? No applause. No trophy. No job promotion.

Defeat. It sucks.

I used to hate it when people told me to learn from a loss, but it's good advice.

Even after the other team celebrates, you can look back on what you did right and say you gave it your best. That's what it's about anyway.

THE STAT SHEET

Players, coaches, and fans love stats. Sportswriters thrive on them.

When the game is over, coaches pore over them and analyze each player's performance. They study them to see where their athletes excelled and where they need to make improvements.

Can a setback be good? What can you learn from a thumping by the other team?

Yes, setbacks can be beneficial. Experience is the best teacher in life. Maybe you got burned on the pick-and-roll. Next game you'll watch for the signs.

You find the will and drive to become more determined.

Perhaps you were passed over for the promotion you wanted.

When the next one rolls around, examine your past performances and figure out what to do differently. Take the initiative and consult with supervisors to develop a plan to strategize your goals. A good coach draws up a game plan, and the players execute it.

Allow your determination to motivate you.

Hold within you the attitude that turns a minor setback into a major comeback.

A loss can awaken the compassionate side in you too. You can relate to others who have experienced similar defeats and help and encourage them.

Never think you're above asking for help and guidance. Productive players will seek advice from their coaches, who in turn are likely passing on information they received from a mentor while growing up.

Keep playing hard. Don't allow one or two losses to ruin the season.

Because before you know it, the referee will toss the ball in the air to begin the next game.

Be ready to win.

Go Big Blue!

How can you learn from a past loss?

WEEK 49 | THE MOST FAMOUS ACL

THEY SAY INJURIES ARE A part of sports. But for Kentucky fans, injuries are the bane of one's existence. In all of Kentucky Basketball's glorious history, how many national championships were taken away because of an inopportune sprained ankle, stress fracture, broken leg, or torn ligament?

Longtime Cat fans will remember Mike Casey breaking his leg in a car accident before the 1969–1970 season. Despite his absence, the Wildcats went on to a 26–2 record and a number-one national ranking before bowing out to Jacksonville in the NCAA regional finals. Casey's backcourt prowess, teamed with Dan Issel and Mike Pratt up front, would have been an unstoppable combination that could have certainly propelled Kentucky to another title run.

Likewise, Sam Bowie's stress fracture in his left tibia could have cost the Cats multiple national championships in the early '80s. Bowie missed nearly two years due to his injury and was never the same when he returned for his senior year. How many teams can lose a 7'1" superstar who can run, jump, shoot, and block shots and say they never missed a beat?

Keith Bogans's sprained ankle cost Kentucky and Tubby Smith a potential national title in 2003. The number-one-ranked Wildcats lost to Marquette in the NCAA regional finals that year when Bogans could barely run or move laterally. With their star player incapacitated, Kentucky was easy pickings for Dwyane Wade and his breakout performance.

But the most agonizing injury for Wildcat fans over the years has to be Derek Anderson's ACL. Prior to going down in the 77–53 win against Auburn on January 18, 1997, the affable 6'5" guard from Louisville was having a stellar season for the highly ranked Wildcats. He was the SEC's leading scorer at 18.6 points per game and led the team in three-point shooting (40.4%), free-throw shooting (80.6%), and steals (2.1 per game). He was a respected team leader, and his injury was a crushing blow.

Not only did Anderson's knee injury cost the Cats the 1997 championship, but since Kentucky brought home the trophy in both 1996 and 1998, it cost the program a three-peat. Plus, the injury lingered over the course of the entire remainder of the 1997 season, causing all of BBN to stress over whether Anderson would make it back in time for the tournament.

Surprisingly, Anderson did make it back in time to get on the court—but not in the way Wildcat fans envisioned. The date was Saturday, March 29, 1997. Kentucky had advanced to another Final Four and was playing Minnesota in the RCA Dome in Indianapolis. When Gophers head coach Clem Haskins was assessed a technical foul in the second half, Rick Pitino signaled Anderson from off the bench to shoot the free throws. Anderson swished them both as Kentucky advanced to the final game with a 78–69 victory.

Although Anderson was cleared by doctors to play two nights later against Arizona in the championship tilt, there was no way Rick Pitino was going to risk further injury and Anderson's professional career by putting him in harm's way.

History will record that the 47,028 folks in attendance on the night of March 31, 1997, saw Arizona defeat Kentucky 84–79 in overtime. But every Wildcat fan knows that there's no way Arizona wins if Derek Anderson had been in the lineup that night.

THE TWISTED ANKLE

Injuries always seem to happen at the most inopportune times.

There is never a good time for an injury, and setbacks usually appear when they are least welcomed or when there is a big game on the line.

You might be facing some large financial struggles when the car breaks down.

Or maybe you or a family member have health issues and suddenly your job is at risk due to a plant shutdown with the potential to affect your health benefits.

Or you may be on your way to a job interview, and you get stuck in unexpected traffic.

Just when you seem to have climbed out from one hole, you are shoved back into another by unexpected circumstances.

Problems can appear to pile up on you, and that nagging injury will keep you off the court.

Doubt and fear can sneak their way into your thoughts and keep you up at night.

LACE UP THE BRACES

Setbacks, injuries, and illnesses can invite discouragement and confusion.

The last thing you need is another bill or a stay in the hospital.

Stumbling blocks can steal your joy and happiness and put you in an overall bad mood.

Keep pushing, play through the pain, and adjust. Keep the passion alive and prepare to the best of your ability. Coaches must be ready to adjust a game plan and call on a bench player when the star goes down. Always be ready to adapt to your surroundings.

You might have to go against the grain for a while, but the experiences you will value later in life will come from challenging times. Growth is a good thing, and while medicine may taste bad going down, it will help you to heal.

When you struggle, take your mind off your problems by helping someone else in need. Others have problems too, but you can be a light and provide encouragement to someone going through a dark valley.

Focus on what you can control. You are in charge of your effort and your attitude. Break down tasks into manageable pieces and complete them one step at a time.

Keep a positive attitude and rely on your faith.

It's okay to talk to your pastor or seek advice and comfort from a higher power. That will provide inner strength for you to endure your situation.

Don't make failure an option. Use defeat as a motivator for the next game. Accept responsibility and believe in your talents and abilities.

Take on each challenge and be prepared to play injured for a while.

You can win the game when the buzzer sounds. And when you do, that pain will slowly fade away.

Go Big Blue!

How can you battle during a setback? How can you adjust your game plan and priorities?

_____

_____

_____

_____

WEEK 50 | FIRST IN LINE

WHEN IT COMES TO ALL-AMERICANS recognized by the NCAA, the University of Kentucky has an impressive number of basketball players populating the current list—as of 2020, sixty-three to be exact, according to the Kentucky Men's Basketball Record Book. Of those players, twenty-one have been named consensus First Team All-America twenty-six total times. From Ralph Beard, Dan Issel, and Kyle Macy to Jamal Mashburn, John Wall, and Anthony Davis, the parade of Wildcat greats is resplendent and regal.

The initial member of the Kentucky All-American club was none other than Basil Hayden. Born on May 19, 1899, the Paris, Kentucky, native lived to the ripe old age of 103. In 1921—his All-American season at UK—Hayden, a 5'11" guard-forward, averaged 9.6 points per game and captained the Wildcat squad that, on March 1 in the Atlanta Municipal Auditorium, beat Georgia 20–19 in the finals of the Southern Intercollegiate Athletic Association Championship. The SIAA was a forerunner to the SEC, and their tournament was possibly the first college basketball tournament ever played—and Kentucky's first significant basketball championship.

Hayden's achievements as a player didn't quite transfer over to his coaching résumé. After graduation from UK and a couple of abbreviated stints in the business world, Hayden accepted the challenge of coaching the UK basketball team. Unfortunately, he only had a week to prepare with what he claimed were "a bunch of scrubs—players who had played in the YMCA and church leagues mostly"—left over from his predecessor, Ray Eklund.

What resulted in that 1926–1927 season was a dismal 3–13 record, giving Basil Hayden the distinction of being the least successful coach in UK Basketball history.

Hayden's successor, John Mauer, went on to a combined 40–14 record in his three years at the UK helm before turning the reins over to a twenty-nine-year-old, up-and-coming coach from Kansas named Adolph Rupp.

There's a first for everything, and Basil Hayden could never have known the cavalcade of great players who would follow in his footsteps. For longtime UK Basketball fans, the mere mention of names like Alex Groza, "Wah Wah" Jones, Bill Spivey, Frank Ramsey, Cliff Hagan, Bob Burrow, and "Cotton" Nash is enough to trigger a boatload of precious memories.

Similarly, ask any True Blue fan to tell you a personal tale about Louie Dampier, Kevin Grevey, Jack Givens, Sam Bowie, Kenny Walker, Tony Delk, or Tayshaun Prince, and they'll most likely talk your ear off.

Even among the younger generation of fans, stories involving a Michael Kidd-Gilchrist, Julius Randle, Tyler Ulis, Jamal Murray, Malik Monk, De'Aaron Fox, or P. J. Washington will invariably bring out a heaping helping of millennial pleasure and pride.

All these All-Americans accomplished great things on the basketball court while playing for the Blue and White. Many of them went on to distinguished professional careers and left behind long-lasting personal legacies. They're all part of the greatest tradition in the history of college basketball. And they're all descended from Basil Hayden—the first in the Big Blue line of All-American greats at the University of Kentucky.

TRYOUTS

Who doesn't want to be successful? No one wakes up each morning and says, "I think I'll just be mediocre today. I don't have any ambition, and I don't want to be productive."

You can control your attitude and effort, whether it's your first day of college, your first day on the job, or your first date with the person of your dreams. Your journey must begin somewhere.

Maybe you come from a background where you did not enjoy the finer things in life and you had to scrape for everything you got. Perhaps you hailed from a modest home, and your parents were able to fulfill your basic needs, but there was nothing extra. But if they taught you the difference between right and wrong, as well as how to maintain a solid work ethic, you are wealthier than you realize, and you can go on to achieve greatness.

MAKE THE TEAM

A fresh start is a good way to examine your goals and dreams before you pursue them. Take the time to make a list of what you want to accomplish.

It's okay to dream big and reach for the stars. You won't get there if you don't. But it's also practical to have a backup plan.

The first thing you need to do is take action. If you want to go to college, apply for admission and sign up for classes. If you want to become an entrepreneur, find the problem you want to solve and seek the advice of those who have already found success starting their own businesses.

Stop overthinking your plans and execute. When players are in the "zone," they just shoot. They don't analyze. Create the plan. Come off the pick and take the shot.

Opportunities will open up when you start to take action. If you fail, get up and try again, but learn from your mistakes and turnovers.

You may not see the win immediately. Your journey may take months or even years. Be prepared to be patient.

Make sure you surround yourself with good people—a buddy who can't keep a job or has relationship issues might not be the best person to ask for advice.

Examine the group you hang with. Good community is important.

Ask yourself if those you surround yourself with make you successful or not. When you are around positive people who will push you and hold you accountable, you are on the right track.

Network and mingle; find people who inspire and encourage you to be your best.

Always make room for improvements. Read more and seek to educate yourself. Be open to new ideas and do your own research.

Reading strengthens your mind and helps reduce stress levels. Read books and articles that will help you reach your goals or make you curious.

Don't be afraid to take a risk, and always invest time in *you* every day. You should put others first, but also dedicate some time for yourself and your family each day.

Treat yourself to a cup of coffee in the morning and meditate on your plans.

Be grateful for what you have and maintain a positive mind-set.

This will help to prepare you to accomplish great things in life. Become an All-American. Enjoy the journey.

Go Big Blue!

Where can you start? What plans do you have?

WEEK 51 | THE GRUDGE

KEVIN GREVEY WAS A TWO-TIME All-American, a three-time First Team All-SEC selection, and a two-time SEC Player of the Year during his storied basketball career at the University of Kentucky. The 6'5" southpaw from Hamilton, Ohio, had a jump shot that he could bury from anywhere on the court. That sweet stroke carried Grevey to 1,801 career points, which ranks him seventh on the all-time UK scoring list.

Before he racked up all those scoring accolades, Grevey played on the most famous UK freshman team ever assembled. That 1971–1972 team, coached by Joe B. Hall and consisting of the heralded recruiting class of Jimmy Dan Conner, Jerry Hale, Mike Flynn, G. J. Smith, Steve Lochmueller, Bob Guyette, and Grevey, went on to an undefeated 22–0 season, routing their opponents by an average margin of victory of 32.8 points per game. Grevey led the precocious freshmen in scoring with a 22.2 points per game average.

But it wasn't just his prowess on the hardwood that made Grevey popular with True Blue fans. No—there were two other qualities about Grevey that have endeared him to BBN forever.

First of all, Grevey had that charismatic personality that people naturally gravitate to. Everybody wanted to be his friend.

The guy liked to have fun, and regardless of how much trouble he got himself into, he was always able to extricate himself through the sheer force of his personality and charm.

Second, Grevey never forgave UCLA coach John Wooden for announcing his retirement before the 1975 NCAA championship game. Longtime Wildcat fans remember that well, and many agree with Grevey that it cost Kentucky dearly. On March 31, 1975, before 15,151 fans at the San Diego Sports Arena, UCLA defeated Kentucky 92–85 for their tenth national title. Grevey led all scorers that night with 34 points in a game he swears to this day Kentucky should have won.

During that game, Kentucky surged out to an early 6-point lead, only to have UCLA fight back and lead 43–40 at the half. In the second half, UCLA still held an 8-point lead at the twelve-minute mark before Kentucky made a run that cut the deficit to 1 with five minutes to play. With the help of some questionable officiating, UCLA was able to hold on to give Wooden his parting retirement gift—another championship ring.

After his UK career, Grevey was drafted number eighteen overall in the first round of the 1975 NBA draft by the Washington Bullets. He went on to have a productive ten-year professional career averaging 17.4 points over 672 games.

Many years later, Grevey still held a grudge against Wooden, claiming that announcing his retirement right before the championship game was a selfish thing to do. It put the spotlight on the coach and not on the team. Furthermore, it resulted in a banner that rightfully belonged in the rafters of Rupp Arena now mistakenly hanging in Pauley Pavilion.

That's an egregious error that all Wildcat fans find hard to live with—a grudge that Kevin Grevey will rightfully never let die down.

THE SECOND-HALF RUN

Oftentimes, holding a grudge is not healthy.

Inevitably, someone will hurt you either personally or professionally. You are not immune to it, so be ready. You won't get a warning when a coworker is about to stab you in the back or your significant other dumps you out of the blue.

Holding a grudge can haunt you and hinder your progress.

Bitterness can invite health issues and keep you up at night. It can affect your mood and give you a negative outlook on life. You might become paranoid and find it difficult to trust people going forward.

But are there any good aspects of holding a grudge?

THE POSTGAME PRESSER

Letting go of frustrations can be a challenge. There is no time limit or instructions to follow—only your gut instincts.

However, a grudge can sometimes serve as a form of protection, causing you to reflect and keep from making another turnover.

A healthy grudge may lead you to establish helpful boundaries for the future. Parameters can sometimes keep you inbounds and protect you from future penalties.

This does not mean you should withdraw or hide, but you will learn not to allow others to take advantage of you moving forward.

Don't seek revenge but be aware of those who set you up or take advantage of you to promote themselves. Set the pick and draw the charge instead.

A grudge can also empower or motivate you to succeed.

You never want to do something for spite, but sometimes proving to a person that they were wrong can boost you to the next level.

Turn your negative thoughts into motivation.

And once you have reached that milestone, don't flaunt or brag, but enjoy your new inner sense of accomplishment.

A publisher once told me that I would never be a published author. When one of my books later won an award, he was there to witness it. I strolled by and shook his hand and said it was nice to see him.

My point was made, and I acted like a gentleman. But I walked away with quiet fulfillment.

A grudge can be a good thing if it's used the right way.

Use it to reflect and to motivate. Never use it to harvest emotions, get even, or promote hard feelings.

And never hold on to those feelings for too long. Forgive but don't forget. Use the grudge, but toss it into the dirty laundry basket to be cleaned up after the game.

Go Cats!

How can you turn a grudge into something positive?

_____

_____

_____

_____

_____

_____

_____

_____

_____

_____

_____

_____

WEEK 52 | IT'S GOTTA BE THE FANS

WHY DOES KENTUCKY BASKETBALL GENERATE so much passion? There's really only one correct answer: *it's gotta be the fans!* From Pikeville to Paducah—or from Puerto Rico to Panama for that matter—die-hard University of Kentucky fans worldwide live and die with the fortunes of their beloved Wildcats. It's a well-known fact that moods, productivity, and relationships within the Big Blue Nation are all tied in to whether the Cats win or lose. Those gut-wrenching defeats bring out the worst in all of us. But whenever that last shot goes in, suddenly *all is well with my soul.*

What's the reason for this unbridled passion? It all stems from our heritage and culture. It's that deep pleasure and satisfaction derived from having your identity tied in with the program—the program with the greatest tradition in the history of college basketball. Fans in other states cheer on their team. Kentucky fans are *invested* in their team and the program. There's an ownership, kinship, and brotherhood that's hard to explain. It's like family—or as John Calipari calls it, "La Familia." Once a Wildcat, always a Wildcat.

I've heard it explained this way. Kentucky is a small state. Other than bourbon, horses, and fried chicken, there's not a whole lot about the Bluegrass State that citizens of the commonwealth can brag about. For many, life is a grind. The one thing we do know, however, is that we're good at basketball. When Kentucky Basketball is relevant and competing for championships, life's hardships just don't seem to hurt quite as much anymore. Regardless of race, socioeconomic status, or political viewpoints, Kentucky fans have that common bond—an inherent passion to somehow will their team to victory and to let the rest of the basketball world know how much they care.

Kentucky fans are knowledgeable, dedicated, and loyal to a fault. Say anything remotely negative about the team and be prepared to face the wrath of an angry BBN. When disaster hits the program—like it did in the Billy Gillispie years or after a pandemic-shortened season—Kentucky fans are hurt and embarrassed. They'll circle the wagons, go into protective mode, and come back more passionate than ever.

UK coach John Calipari frequently speaks of the "Kentucky Effect," whereby the Wildcats not only move the needle but *are* the needle in the world of college basketball. He believes that pushing and promoting his players to always achieve the highest standards possible is the best and only way to affect the entire game.

There's a "Kentucky Effect" among UK fans too. They're pushing for excellence and promoting themselves as the best fans in the world. They want to influence the game. They proudly don their colors and travel everywhere in support of their team, swallowing the other schools' fans up in a vortex of blue. They call it the blue mist. Just like the 2012 SEC tournament in "Blue Orleans"—once you've been a part of it, you'll never forget what it was like.

But above all, Wildcat fans care ultimately about winning—about beating Duke, North Carolina, Kansas, Louisville, and UCLA—and about championship banners hanging in the rafters of Rupp Arena.

That glorious heritage and tradition is part of their DNA. They wear it like a badge of honor and pass it down from generation to generation. Because when it comes right down to it, Kentucky fans love their Cats. But they love beating your team even more. That's a winning combination . . . and the secret to Kentucky passion!

THE OPENING TIP

Life can be challenging and full of discouragements at times. Circumstances out of your control can blindside you if you are not careful, and they can utterly take the wind out of you.

Surprises may come in many varieties and often without warning.

A basketball team can have a 20-point lead and before they know it, the opponent has trimmed the spread to only 6 points with five minutes to play.

In the blink of an eye, you can be staring at an upset in life.

At that point, you have two options: accept defeat or play harder.

In order to enjoy the game of life, one thing is essential.

One attribute must be present and must remain bright.

THE BIG WIN!

Passion.

According to Webster's Dictionary, it's defined as a strong and barely controllable emotion.

Burnout is going to come, but you must be able to reignite the burning flame within your soul to be victorious.

There are ways to keep your passion alive and well. It is not only vital in the workplace; it's a must in life.

You don't have to love your job to have a deep passion for life, but it is extremely helpful.

You can be unemployed, laid off, or in a temporary hunt for a career and still have a zeal and zest for life.

You have to—for yourself and for those you love.

You also have to pick yourself up after a loss, get back in the gym, and watch game film to prepare for the next contest.

Set short-term goals that will lead you along a clear path to the hoop to reach your long-term ambitions.

You can't score 120 points if you don't score one, two, or three at a time.

See the big picture and strike a balance. Come up with a game plan to chip away and put points on the board.

But also take risks and put together a full-court press to keep the other team honest.

Get out of your comfort zone and do something out of character. Go somewhere you have never been before or take an alternate route to work. Mix things up.

And it's okay to take a break to recharge.

This might mean unplugging from your social media accounts, turning off your phone, or not reading emails over the weekend.

Find your happy place and surround yourself with positive people that you love who will encourage and support you.

This book has stressed repeatedly that the two things you can control are your attitude and your effort, but to control those attributes, you must possess the desire—you must have and demonstrate the passion.

That is what makes UK Basketball fans the best in the world, and that will be the reason you live the best life possible—with *passion*.

Go Big Blue!

How can you live with passion?

CONCLUSION

I BELIEVE I SPEAK FOR John when I say that I hope you have been inspired over the past fifty-two chapters of *Kentucky Passion*.

We tried to put together a mixture of fond memories of wonderful athletes who made fantastic plays along with a few history lessons too.

John's assignment was to relive the moments of UK greatness, and he did that with such brilliance. He told the stories in a way that took you back in time and made you feel like you were sitting in the bleachers watching the history all over again.

His passion for Kentucky Basketball is obvious.

He is a fan and an unapologetic member of Big Blue Nation.

My portions of the book came after John's vivid descriptions in each chapter. I had to take what he put down on paper and find a way to tie it in to everyday life and try to motivate and inspire.

But in order for me to do that, I had to read and take in every word John wrote.

Over the years as a sportswriter, I "knew enough" about the Cats. I had my own opinions about certain players and coaches. But reading what John had to say caused me to rethink my long-held positions and entertain a different view.

I was inspired. His contagious passion spills out and splashes over the reader.

Throughout this book, I learned more about Kentucky Basketball than I ever knew before.

I always knew the members of BBN were loyal to their team. But I never really understood it until I worked together with John on this project.

When I was in junior high school many years ago, one of my teachers was a die-hard UK fan. That was my first real exposure to a dedicated follower of the team.

The Wildcat faithful have a reason to celebrate and cheering for their team is a way of life. There are no lukewarm supporters. You are either in or out.

BBN is a family—an enormous community that spans the world over.

To its followers, Kentucky Basketball is much more than a team. It's more than wins and losses. There is a distinct dedication and tradition like no other.

Every fan is just as much a part of each victory and national championship as the players are.

And the same goes for those rare occasions when a loss is experienced. Hearts are broken, but they're often repaired by the next game. They are truly resilient.

The word *passion* has a simple definition. It means to have a "strong and barely controllable emotion."

Other teams have fans. But Kentucky Basketball followers are different. Their strong emotions run deep, and they demonstrate a unique passion other teams don't possess.

John and I hope you enjoyed your motivational and inspirational journey with BBN.

I truly have a new appreciation for Kentucky Basketball and its family of fans. I know why they are passionate about the program. It's more than winning and losing. It's about loyalty, integrity, and tradition.

It's all about passion. It's *Kentucky Passion*.

Go Big Blue.

Del Duduit